THE
BUSINESS
OF
CONNECTION

An ENE Anthology

National Library of Australia Cataloguing-in-Publication data:
The Business of Connections
Success/Self-help

ISBN: (sc) 978-0-6489847-6-4
ISBN: (e) 978-0-6450155-3-9

CONTENTS

It all began at a castle in Northern Ireland, business owners from all over the globe gathered...

...now their stories that elevated their business & lives is all in ONE BOOK!

Steve Jobs said it best, "...you can't connect the dots looking forward; you can only connect them looking backward. So you have to trust that the dots will somehow connect in your future."

...and now you can learn what those "dots" were in the lives of nearly 30 business owners from all over the globe...

...from an nearly 80 year old dairy woman, to home-builder, to a publisher currently publishing for the Duchess of York, to the Countess & Lord of Erne...and yes, even my story. I love to say I am just a Grandma from Idaho. Let's see where these dots take you.

Dots That Connect To Your Future

Steve Jobs has a saying, "You can't connect the dots looking forward, you can only connect them looking backwards. So you will have to trust that the dots somehow connect to your future."

Here's the funny thing, the dots that connect to our futures are sometimes disguised in the strangest ways...sometimes in the shape of a potato!

My first business was selling dirty Idaho (USA) potatoes out of my minivan. My five children could be seen waving a homemade poster. Why we even coached our five-year-old to run from crosswalk to crosswalk pushing the walk button to stop traffic in front of our little potato station beside the road.

We would mostly get permission from our city, but mostly not. There were many a day when the police would stop us and ask if we had permission to be out there. Oh dear! "No, sorry officer."

This part of my business life was the beginning of a 10-year evolution of business, learning and knowledge that has now taken me to renting a castle in Northern Ireland with the publisher of this book! These dots in our lives, they certainly connect now, but when you are in the middle of it, there is just no way to see where they are going.

So how in the world does a mom from Idaho, USA (which, FYI, is one state in from the west coast of the USA, and only about two hours from the amazing Yellowstone National park... yep! Bears and all!) end up renting a Castle in Northern Ireland with the epic Karen Mc Dermott?

Well, let me tell you, it's one "yes" at a time, one new beginning at a time, and one dot at a time.

That little minivan dot soon turned into a large moving van, that I (get this) became, "That Potato Lady." Yes! We decaled that van with my thatpotatolady email address and MY PERSONAL CELL number. Can you believe it?

Soon that large moving van evolved into dot number 3, opening two lovely Farmer's Markets, complete with nearly 100 venders, along the river, cobblestone streets and all. Every hour, on the hour, bagpipers would march down the cobblestone streets of Idaho Falls, Idaho. I can smell the cinnamon donuts cooking now!

As the growth of our children happened as well as our opportunities, dot number 3 became dot number 4, a fundraising company. We soon were shipping produce from three states into five states in the US. Eventually we hit the goal of earning $1 million for school sports teams, clubs, and bands. Kids were earning much needed funds to march in the coveted Macy's day parade in New York, a famous children's choir went to Paris, all from selling dirty Idaho potatoes, California oranges, and Washington Apples.

I know you are wondering; how does the fundraising dot connect to the Castle dot? Well, it doesn't! Ha! At least not directly, but for sure it does indirectly.

You see, we had brokers working for us in various US cities to represent our Fundraising company to the schools. A mutual contact (here comes your dot) of one of our brokers was opening an Executive Networking membership. My broker said, "You should get to know Shelly Yorgesen. She seems to know everyone."

Truth be told, at this point, I didn't really know that many people. Sure, we had a great Farmer's Market list, and city contacts, (oh and yes, we received permission of the city for our fun). But my network was NOTHING compared to what it was about to become.

One day out of the blue, I received an email from said gentleman that mentioned this networking group he was wanting to open. I honestly felt swamped with a young, large family, the Farmers Markets, and Fundraising company, and had no idea what he was talking about in his email.

Networking? Was this a network marketing invite? I really had no idea what he was talking about! I, at this point in my life had never done any "formal" networking, this was a new concept to me, and one I had zero experience with...so I deleted his email, and the next one, and then finally, the 3rd time he emailed me, I finally opened it. The reason I opened it is the reason I do most everything in my life. I simply "felt" like I should.

This little prompting from above has never mis-lead me, I try to always stay in tune to the whispers from heaven.

I read the email, we met, and I agreed to help him open his new business. We grew a membership in our local city & opened a second chapter in our capital city about 4 hours away. My involvement in this executive membership was a beautiful journey that changed everything about me.

Turns out, when you spend nearly a decade of your life finding ways to help fancy people grow their businesses, by truly listening to their needs, learning what they were struggling with, and then connecting them to each other is really good for you. I became the connector, the person who knew the struggles of all these business owners and soon a trusted super connector.

Changing who you know & who you spend your time with changes everything in your life. They say. "you are the average of the 5 people you spend the most time with." This is 100% true for me and the new path in life I had taken.

Opportunities opened to me that involved being awarded "Best Air Show" by the US Naval Blue Angel's. Let me tell you, that was an experience! To being contracted with an international company to host a Centennial Celebration for their company. This event included producing a movie, writing a book, and even hosting a concert. My goodness, dot number 4…buckle up, I tell you. You never know to what heights you will climb.

Dot number 5…

I have come to the conclusion that not all dots are created equal. Some grow you faster, some take you farther, some terrify you, but all are there in order, and for a grand design. You, like me, have just one job, and that is to say "yes" to the dots as they arise. The journey is yours to take, but only if you grab the dots as they appear.

Dot number 5 is how we get to the castle with fancy Karen. You see, this is where my networking career really changes me, forever. For a decade now, I have led live executive networking events. Gathering fancy people into one space to help them learn to collaborate, to problem solve and to open doors for each other.

About six years into this dot, I had the thought, what if I could gather international business minds, business owners from all corners of the globe? Dropping the boundaries of my city, my state, even my country…and that is when Karen Mc Dermott came into my world. Karen quickly became a member of my first global membership, a networking experience for women in business.

We met monthly, women from Australia to Florida, from Canada to California. Karen's shining smile and unreal talent for publishing soon got her on my "virtual stage." After listening to her passion for publishing our stories, she and I decided we needed to host an event together.

And so you have it, magical dot number 6. A castle in her hometown in Northern Ireland. A dream for any business owner. And a castle, brimming with business owners, executives and CEOs from eight countries, growing their businesses, growing personally, and yes, even growing me.

So, what is dot number 7? What could possibly be next? Well, that same Karen girl got me to author a book for my Non-Profit called "Operation Christmas Magic." A dot that makes all dots happy. And so, dot number 7 becomes a book. Operation Christmas Magic, The Real Mrs. Claus Story. See, I told you this dot makes all dots happy!

And so, what is your next dot? Well, I wish I could tell you. The best I can tell you is, say "yes" to crazy things. Yes to potatoes, yes to cobblestones, yes to band groups, and yes to castles. Say yes to your dots. Here they come. I hope you enjoy the stories of connections with it this amazing book.

Many of these business owners within the cover of this book attended the castle event with us. Most of them have never been an author before, and you are enjoying their next "dot" with them in their journey.

Most of these business owners (now authors) are members of our global membership for business owners, executives, coaches & consultants.

Should you wish to join us, we would love to meet you, and possibly become the next dot to your future.

Connect with us at www.executivenetworkingevents.com

SHELLY YORGESEN is a power-connector, and believes your future success is probably hiding in the next person you meet.

Her first business was actually selling dirty Idaho potatoes out of the back of her minivan, on the streets of Idaho USA! Yes! Selling ice to Eskimos!

...and now 10 years later, after finding her real super-power in helping high-level leaders connect, she actually rented a Castle in Northern Ireland and filled it with Executives from 8 countries for an *International Executive Networking Symposium.*

Having led high-end executive networking events for nearly a decade, she took her expertise of connecting high-level executives & business owners into the online space. She has created a global executive networking membership for executives & business owners called *The Executive Networking Events Inner Circle.*

The Inner Circle meets monthly online & grants you access to diverse perspectives from a wide range of industry leaders from many countries across the globe.

The mission of the ENE Inner Circle is to help business owners in 3 areas: Grow global connections, learn how to navigate the online space & give high-level growth strategies to scale business.

Shelly is the also the President of Operation Christmas Magic her non-profit that makes Christmas Miracles happen from Africa to Idaho.

She says she's just a "Grandma from Idaho"...that is her favorite title ever!

MARILYN FORESTER

Connections Down
on the Farm

1960 – 2020, with Dwain And Marilyn Forester

How does a girl born in Los Angeles, who spent as much time as possible at the beach, end up running a dairy with 1000 dairy cattle? And retire at age seventy-eight, with her husband, with no debt while still owning the farm ground, new cars and a large home?

Well, here is my story, which is also our story. My family moved from Southern California to Northern California after I graduated from Inglewood High School. I started college at Shasta

Jr College. I applied for a job as a secretary at the local employment office because I could type and take shorthand. Mildred Doty had a different idea. She needed a full charge bookkeeper and didn't care that I only had one semester of same in high school. She was my first connection and taught me how to run an office, do billing, and keep books. All knowledge that was critical when we began running our own business.

I was a football song leader and made friends with a mutual friend of my husband-to-be. She introduced us. It was love at first sight for me. Dwain Forester was in the Air Force at the time and lived in a town near Redding where I lived. I guess you could say my friend Helen was my second connection.

So, city girl married future farm boy. It was tough going on the farm, so husband took a winter job helping an old school buddy build a dairy parlor. This did not seem pivotal at the time, but you will see later that it was. Things improved, and we bought a beautiful farm on the edge of the Modoc National Forest in a little town in North Eastern California called Cedarville. There we raised four natural and three adopted children. Husband was a very hard worker who made friends easily. We acquired a second farm and trucked our hay out of the mountains a great distance. We farmed there for eighteen years, when the next major connection surfaced. Our farm was the bench mark farm for the bank we financed with, which meant they compared all other farms in the area to our farm. They also monitored the water in our wells and found the water depth was steadily lowering. If it continued, the land values would fall. We'd become good friends with the loan officer, who made us aware of the water issue.

Along came the next connection. His name was Vern Marble, and he was the head of the Agronomy Dept. at the University of California at Davis. Dwain asked him where he would go if he were going to buy a farm. He said, "Columbia Basin in Washington State, hands down." And that is what we did. We sold both California farms and bought a 640-acre hay farm in the Columbia Basin in 1979. We built a new home and continued raising our seven children in Washington State. Now that date would mean nothing to you unless you lived in Washington on May 18, 1980. The Mount Saint Helens volcano erupted at 8 am that morning and covered our ready-to-harvest crop with an inch and a quarter of volcanic ash. Not good. It also didn't help that interest rates in the mid-80s for agricultural loans were as high as 22%. Long story short, we filed for a newly developed for farmers, Chapter 12 bankruptcy in 1986.

We found our next connection through a newspaper article about an attorney located seventy miles from us. He was making the Chapter 12 bankruptcy his specialty. We contacted him; he took our case as his model case. He took the case pro bono, and we successfully completed all that was required of us. We reduced our acres to 147, and gave back the remainder to the original owner after investing a great deal of money in the irrigation system.

I know this sounds depressing, but Dwain now says it was the best thing that could have happened to us. It definitely didn't seem that way at the time. Remember that dairy barn building experience husband had that I mentioned earlier? Well, now it becomes important. It is not possible to make a living on 147 acres, so determined husband, (with wife kicking and screaming) trades hay for eighty head of small dairy heifers from a person to whom he shipped hay. He then amassed equipment to put in a dairy barn by buying from one of the many dairies that were going out to business at the time. He jackhammered out part of the floor in our existing shop and built a milking barn. We learned to milk cows by being mentored by the guy for whom he built that original dairy barn. We milked cows for thirty-one years and acquired three neighboring farms along the way. Farming is like gambling, and so there were many not so good years and a few good years.

We connected with other successful dairy people and learned how to do it right. I ran the dairy, did all the books, kept the right amount of feed on hand, and husband kept it running, and did the farming. We focused on building a healthy, productive herd, and raising children who knew how to work, and paying down debt. I used to joke our milk cows were our 401K's. This turned out to be true and not a joke. Health issues affected my eighty-year-old Dwain, and so he agreed we should sell. There was a local large dairyman who, four years prior to the sale, told us he was going to buy our cows.

At the time he told us, we were not at all interested. He and his two brothers were ready when we were ready. Had we remained as a hay farm, and not had the volcanic tragedy, we would not have been able to retire with an income from selling our 401K cows. Or leasing out the farm, financing the equipment we sold to the buyers, and selling various equipment the cow buyers didn't buy. And we still own our home and the farm.

Dwain had served twenty-two years on the board of the Washington State Dairy Federation and simultaneously on the board of the nation's largest dairy coop, Dairy Farmers of America. He'd connected with dairy farmers across the U. S., and we enjoyed the extremely informative DFA annual meetings. This all ended. After a few weeks of retirement, said ambitious husband, became depressed. I told him he needed a hobby. He'd worked all those years with no time to develop a one. There was one hobby he had before we moved up to Washington, which was flying his Cessna 182 airplane. Sadly this plane had to be sold during the bankruptcy.

Bet you can guess what his new hobby is. At 82 years old, he took down all the corrals, bought a track hoe at an auction, and took out all the cement feed aprons. Then he built a runway and turned the part of the loafing barn (where cows sleep and eat), that we did not sell, into a hanger. He is now the proud owner of a 175B Cessna airplane, which he can see from his dining room table, and not be bored.

So many people we connected with along the way had an influence on our comfortable retirement. Work hard, pay down debt and do all that you can do, and the Lord will do the rest.

MARILYN FORESTER: I feel somewhat intimidated to be in the presence of so many successful business people.

I do have an honor to claim that none of you can tout. I am the mother of Shelly and the grandmother of Jordelle. Something I am truly proud of.

My story of connections is somewhat unique.

It's about a city girl from the suburbs of Los Angeles who meets her prince charming and learns to be a farmer's wife. And then one step further learning how to run a 1000 cow dairy.

It's like the late Steve Jobs of Apple said, *You can't tell where you are going without looking back to connect the dots.* My story connects the dots to get us where we landed a comfortable retirement in a business that does not always end up that way.

MARK REYNOLDS

Mark Reynolds, can you share with us a story of a connection that elevated your business?

Good question. That leads into my philosophy of what life is in general, much less business and that is caring. You have to show up. The people who really get places, it's not because of some strategy, it's not because of some plan or skill set, it's because they show up in life. Many people think they show up, but they really don't show up on purpose, and there's what I mean by showing up, and doing things on purpose. And then if you want to go to a different level, it's separating people who do things on purpose by those who do things with intent. And also, that distinguishes getting places in life, regardless of what plan or methodologies or strategies they have, it's doing things on purpose. It's showing up and going big.

Instead of sitting on the frontage road when the highway of life is right in front of you, always planning. You can hand the map or the tablet to the person in the passenger seat next to you. I know we're not done planning. I know we haven't got it all figured out yet, but I'm getting on that highway anyway and turning in the correct direction and simply going. We are mostly ready so what are we waiting for?

I'm not waiting. I'm showing up. I'll figure it out as I go. And it's those people who have advantages over everybody else, because of my metaphor that Shelly loves and she used it with other interviews. "If you get on the highway and get up to speed, life will show and offer you things that you never knew existed." And they're in the advertisement. They are billboards on the side of the highway to guide you. Offers and opportunities for you to do or experience.

Like, hey, thirteen kilometers ahead, here's this you can consider, and then nine kilometers ahead, you know, and so on, they keep giving you more information. But in the end, you start thinking that might be it. I think I'm curious. I think I'll take that exit and go see what that's about. And the thing is, you can do that and visit that opportunity for a short period of time and say, "OK, that was nice. I learned a lot and I have more knowledge than before to visit more opportunities along the way."

The thing is, you can get back on the highway. Just because you got off the highway doesn't mean that it doesn't have another on ramp. It's all about enjoying the journey! The marketplace is everywhere, so enjoy the journey.

I mean, it really is a connection for me. For me, it's showing up. Even though you don't know what's next as far as a plan or anything else is like. I may not fully know what to do next, but I'm not standing still and that's what matters. That's why I achieved the amazing things I've done

Yes, I have fun on the journey and see opportunities others may not see. For example, with my previous company, I fell into an industry that didn't even exist at the time. It morphed into the money thing. And the funny thing is that I never intended to be in business for myself, ever, but because I was showing up, I grew that company into the third largest in the world. All because I was looking for a job.

People then started seeing things in me that I didn't see in myself and started offering money to me and going. "OK, if you won't do that for me, can you give me information so I can do it myself?" And I'm like, sure, you know, because it was all here in my head. The next thing I know, I've got this Expedition company that turned into the Adventure industry and then turned into Eco-tourism and more. It was all because I was a trained scientist as a Naturalist and I wanted to go hang out with science research stations around the world. I wanted to go explore. My dream job turned into my dream company.

Connections became important because I was showing up. People started recognizing me because of a skill set, again, because I didn't necessarily see in myself. It Was like, "Well, hey Mark, can you do this or can you help me with that?" My thought in my head was, *I'm not sure*, but verbally, I said, "Absolutely!"

So, I found myself in a situation here in 2002 when Washington, D.C., our nation's capital, asked me to come speak to the League of Nations. After one of my two-and-a-half hour workshops to these nation leaders from around the world, I got off the stage for some water because I used up all my water on this stage. I became surrounded by all these world leaders who were saying, "Mark, I've never heard any kind of perspective like that."

It really impressed them.

One guy followed me over to where I could get some water. And he's introduced himself, but when I get off stage, I need some time to decompress my thoughts and my brain hurts at this point because of the speaking and then the listening. And he's like, "So I only have a few hours, but I'd like to see if I could buy you dinner."

Well, I already had thirty-six offers, you know, just getting from the stage over to the water. I'm like, well, that's fine. Then he said, and this is where it got my attention, "I think you are the person we've been looking for who we didn't think existed. That could actually help our country," and I'm like, *who did you say you are?*

He repeated, "I'm the governor over the Samoan islands." And I'm like, *Really?* And he said, "Well, don't you think you have something that you could help us welcome them like in?" Again, in my mind, I'm going, *But I'm not sure*, but verbally, I said, "Absolutely," and I said it with confidence. That's what I mean by showing up and suddenly I've got a great connection.

And that connection led to another country, to another country, to another country, and Washington, D.C. is going, "Can you come back?" So, all I'm saying is connections and opportunities happen because you show up. But you have to do it intentionally. Yes, it's not by accident. I mean, some things are up to the universe or accident or just luck, but not as much as people think. Opportunities are created for me and it all starts with showing up intentionally. Period.

The thing is, when you discover your own purpose, when you live through that, your connections are so much more powerful. And then opportunities become more fluid and suddenly you don't have to try so hard.

MARK REYNOLDS: Between the United States and France, I'm a Business Strategist who works with companies from start-up, to multi-location Corporations in need in becoming more efficient, dominating their industry, developing a predictable monthly profit system , setting predictable benchmark goals that are sustainable and getting actual results. Period.

I have been fortunate enough to speak to the league of Nations in Washington D.C. on business development and operations, have worked all levels of Companies, international Government entities, and Municipal Cities on some level. I have also been a visiting professor that has spoken to 19 Universities both Stateside and abroad as well as many Association, Organization, and Corporate engagements on the aspects of Business.

I want to work with motivated Company owners or C Suit' executives to significantly improve their efficiencies, operations and sustainability. It's about being the go-to company within your marketplace and not being distracted by competing with others.

I have pa significant background in Adventure Travel and Outdoor Sports, love to sail on the open Sea and have done my crazy bucket list (less one item) by the age of 40 and started over again.

DONNA BATES

The unexpected outcomes of connection

Connections come to us through many means. Personal, Business, Family and pretty much any interaction on the planet we have with human beings, can create a valuable opportunity to connect at any level.

It can be formal or contrived, through a networking organization, introductions from others or mere serendipity. These are my favourite connections. Where simply living with joy and curiosity in relationship with others, creates a divine moment of interaction that can change the course of your life forever.

Over my career, I've cultivated many friendships and

relationships that have generated opportunities simply through being curious about people, their lives, their companies or chatting about the uniqueness of their products and services.

One connection yielded a turning point in my career. I was working as a senior executive at a large multi-national media organization. I was creating a new narrative for a company which organizationally, they weren't ready for, but needed. The project would act as a catalyst to transform the company. Being a visionary or pioneer in any company or industry is difficult, but having to bring others along with you, without the buy-in of others, would be impossible. Connections and networking have inevitably been the "secret sauce" that have meant the success or not of projects.

Being a catalyst for change isn't easy, and this project was one of the most challenging times of my career. Not for the project implementation itself, but for the massive complexities of human interaction across several layers of the company and industry.

Opportunities created themselves through people who were watching what I was doing, what I was achieving and simply through coffee meetings and the mechanics of researching and conducting the project itself. They yielded connections that for me at that time, were pivotal to both the successful outcome of the project and my own self-worth.

These were the unexpected outcomes of day-to-day connection. This is where the magic happens.

I look for the wonder in every connection, and in every ordinary conversation, I look for the extraordinary.

Coming out of a "mundane" project meeting where I was communicating how the project was progressing to the Group's Executive Team, the Group CEO, a mature, suave and charismatic gentleman, and someone whose time and access was precious, asked how I was getting back to my home city. I smiled unexpectantly and said, "Taxi to the airport and flying Qantas." I said goodbye and went to visit his secretary. She was a lovely woman and someone I always dropped in to say hello to when I visited Head Office, and on this occasion to let her know I was leaving and that I would see her in a few weeks.

The meeting had gone really well. I felt energized and excited, and took my small, black trolley bag into the elevator, and walked into the building's marble-lined expanse of the foyer. Just before I got to the front revolving doors, the Group CEO walked up next to me and took my small trolley bag. He walked me out of the building through the revolving doors as we chatted and laughed about funny aspects of the project and exchanged pleasantries about what we would be doing on the weekend. At that moment, I realized he was handing my small bag to a chauffeur dressed in a smart black suit, like something out of the Transporter. The chauffeur loaded my bag into the boot of the large, long black limousine he was driving, and opened the door for me to get in.

What I hadn't realized, is that after I said goodbye to his secretary, the Group CEO had asked her to cancel my flight and taxi and rebook me onto a flight in the private company jet with him and two of the other Group Executives to fly back to my home city where they would attend a meeting the next day. The chauffeur-driven limousine was just an added perk.

For him, it was a small thing, maybe a reward for good work, a bit of care for the long hours and acknowledgement I would have to wait for several hours for a commercial flight and then flying time back to my home state.

For me, the ability to be delivered onto the tarmac in a limousine, walk a red carpet to the company's private jet, receive a greeting from a flight attendant, who knew my name, offered me champagne and sushi, and lead me to one of only four seats on the plane, was a game-changer.

What he may or may not have recognized, was that under the surface, bubbly positive demeanor, was that in reality I was exhausted. The flights across several time zones to visit project teams in several states, hours of continual pitching, negotiations, ego-stroking, airplane and hotel food that I'd been living on for several months, was taking a toll. And this was a sanctuary, albeit for only the five hours flying time home.

On that flight back, as the Executives chatted amongst themselves, I felt an overwhelming sense of gratitude and peace. Allowing me to feel appreciated, cared for and that my time was valuable, and my work mattered. It also meant they trusted me. Integrity is my number one value, and to even sit amongst this group, to know that I was trusted, and that what was discussed would be kept in the strictest confidence, was important to me.

Everything happens for a reason. In your life, you will come across some of the most interesting people and connections. At the time, it may just be the most important thing in your world or the least important thing in your world. But don't discount those encounters. What may seem insignificant today could yield blessings into the future in a way you could not even possibly imagine.

Carry a sense of wonder and curiosity every day for the people you connect with. You may or may not cross their paths again, but if you do, the results may be serendipitous, and open a door to an opportunity to you that would otherwise have been closed.

DONNA BATES is an multi-award-winning Business & Marketing Strategist. She is a valued contributor to various newspapers and business journals and is regularly interviewed for business podcasts because of her creative, courageous, straight-talking approach to issues affecting businesses and how they grow.

A former Senior Executive working in Media, Marketing, Defence and Finance sectors, Donna carved out her career creating innovative growth projects for more than two decades before trading her corporate business suits for more casual attire, starting her own successful Strategic Planning consultancy and co-founded a Collaborative Co-sharing space helping businesses create growth in any economy.

Now she strives to write gritty, down-to-earth articles and books about issues facing the global business community for leaders who have to navigate the constantly shifting sands of the business arena.

Donna lives in Western Australia with her husband, and an adorable rescue dog that has claimed its space on their couch. For more information about Donna and her company, visit **www.donnabates.com**

An Idea and a Tow Truck

According to Forbes[1], less than one third of family businesses survive the transition from first to second generation ownership. Another 50% don't survive the transition from second to third generation.

Knowing that statistic provided the fuel for my husband and I, third generation owners, to do everything we could not to let down the family business while we were on watch.

Having newly expanded our automotive repair shop, Oswald Service and Repair, to a neighboring city, we were faced with the challenges of all new start-ups. We weren't well known in the

---

1. https://www.forbes.com/sites/aileron/2013/07/31/the-facts-of-family-business/#4c8de1f69884

community; we didn't have an existing clientele, and the locals already had their patterns set for where they received automotive repair.

Basically, we were going into a market where we would have to work at building brand loyalty from the ground up. We were fortunate to hire experienced staff who lived locally and who were known as reputable and talented in the automotive repair business. But we knew that wouldn't be enough to support our investment and grow our presence in this new town.

As experienced business owners, we had implemented all the tried-and-true methods to build a structure that resulted in success. We knew we had systems in place that would give us the best advantage, but we needed customers to come in the doors. We had highly trained and well-paid staff standing around, and our blood pressure was rising as our bank account was falling.

At the same time, our flagship store had more business than it could handle. We were scheduling up to a week out to take care of customers. And in the automotive business, there are few customers who have the patience to wait a week for their car to even be looked at. So, we were losing business as they took their cars elsewhere.

We'd no idea how connection would solve our problem until we bared our soul at our monthly MasterMind group and were given the gift of the obvious.

If you aren't familiar with MasterMind groups, it is a group of individuals who are all invested in you being successful. Each member of the MasterMind owns their fellow member's future victories as they listen to the challenges each face. The members offer suggestions as a third party looking in and based on their own experiences. This setting allows for shared problem solving. As the saying goes, "Two heads are better than one," and multiple heads are even more powerful.

As we attended the group on this day, we were explaining our challenges of building our new business in this new city. We provided all kinds of detail around what we were doing and how we were frustrated that business had not taken off yet. In addition, we shared our difficulties with our flagship location and how we could not meet the needs of the customers because of our schedule being so full. We told them how we were losing business in one location and struggling to get business in our other location.

One solution we shared was expanding our flagship location to be larger so we could accommodate more vehicles, but that was a long-term plan and we needed a quick fix.

Looking back, I can see how obvious the solution was, but at the time we were too "in the weeds" to see it. Too busy at one location, and not enough business at another location. How about taking cars from the flagship location to the new store? It was right there in front of us, but we needed someone else to point it out.

There were two of the members of the group who commented that we use the second location as overflow bays. This suggestion wasn't an entirely new idea. We'd been asking our customers if they would be willing to take their vehicles to our new location for service and the majority of the time they declined. It was understandable. The second location is thirty miles to the north of our flagship store. This would be at least a half an hour's drive and very inconvenient. Not to mention the fact they would be without a vehicle at least thirty miles from home.

Upon hearing this, one individual proposed we offer a complimentary concierge service to transport the vehicles to the second location, thereby putting no extra burden on the customers. That solution was like a lightning bolt of truth as it hit my ears. Instead of the idea of using the new location being a burden to our customers, the addition of a concierge service changed it to be just that, a service!

We immediately went to work putting this plan into place. For the vehicles that could be driven, the plan worked pretty easily. We had a little bump getting our guy back, but with a little coordination, we could time it so there was a repaired vehicle that needed to be returned and so he could drop off and return. The undrivable vehicles presented a bigger problem.

The only solution we could come up with was to put the vehicles on a trailer and haul them to our new location. We had a trailer that was long enough and was, in fact, a car hauler. The idea seemed solid, so we proceeded with trailering cars back and forth. Pulling cars on a trailer is not an ideal set-up for safety and gas mileage. This lasted for two weeks before we knew we would have to do something different.

We were confident that using the new location as an extension of the flagship shop's bays would work, and our two-week trial proved it. Every day we were transporting at least four cars. Those were cars we would have otherwise had to turn away. Armed with that knowledge, we made a significant investment and bought a tow truck. This allowed us to transport two vehicles at a time and to do it safely. The revenue we were making more than covered the expenses of the truck.

Just a month prior, we would have never imagined we would own a tow truck. We were stuck in the traditional ways of what we knew to bring business to our new location. We were experienced business owners and considered ourselves experts in automotive repair and how to run a successful automotive repair business. Yet it took an architect and a web developer to open our eyes.

This is one of several examples I could provide of how connection has positively impacted our business. As third generation business owners, we have far too often found ourselves with our heads down trudging through our business challenges alone. We have learned how powerful connection is to our business, and how finding those individuals who can view our situation with fresh eyes brings clarity that was beyond our capacity to see.

This third generation isn't going anywhere, and we are building our family business even stronger by extending our family to those powerful connections around us. We encourage you to do the same for your business if you want to take it to the next level.

RENAE OSWALD: *Oswald Service and Repair* is a third generation owned independent automotive repair business with locations in Idaho Falls and Rexburg, Idaho.

In addition to the family business, Renae is an RN and is the president of *New Level Leader*, a leadership consulting business. She is the host of *East Idaho Entrepreneurs* podcast and dabbles in entrepreneurship herself owning several small businesses.

Almost Perfect

It is a beautiful thing when people take the time for others.

I have always loved to travel, an expensive hobby I believe I inherited from my parents. Though they were hardworking hay farmers with seven children, they gave us the opportunity to travel almost yearly, across the country to a child's dream land – Disney World.

I remember so often the conversations my parents would have with complete strangers on the airplane rides across the country from Washington state to Florida. I also can't forget the many hours Dad spent speaking to complete strangers he found in the many theme park lines. Those individuals who had some sort of familiar logo on their clothing that was connected to him, didn't know what they were in for with dear, sweet Dad. The laughter that ensued usually was a good sign.

In my observation over time, I learned to see how well my parents conversed with people, and more often than not, the feeling of good will that emanated from it. A lot of these conversations were for the opportunity to make a new acquaintance and see if any similarities could be found. Every once in a while, there was a connection made. Thousands of miles from home, and a connection is made and sometimes those connections became new business opportunities for the farm. You will never know if you don't ask, right?

Fast forward to October 2019, beautiful Crom Castle, Northern Ireland. My love to travel and see the world was granted further when I was blessed with the opportunity to help with the Inaugural launch of ENE's Symposium.

After getting settled into Crom's cozy cottages and spending what felt like a day catching up on sleep, we loaded up in the van to go to dinner. We stopped to pick up two of our guests, Ron Malhotra and his incredible business partner, Caroline Vass. After Caroline took the front seat up front with our trusty driver Bret, Ron seated himself next to me in the middle row. The conversation that began there has changed me forever for the better.

Let me introduce myself. I grew up third of seven children on a hay farm. For me, it was hard work, educational, and just about perfect. Graduating from school, I earned my way through college with academic scholarships. I married my incredible husband at nineteen, and began our family with our eldest boy, born just over a year after our wedding. However, that did not stop me from completing my education. I pushed forward with my studies and still earned my way through my four-year degree, after having our second boy—just six months before graduating with my Bachelor of

Science. I even had the blessed opportunity to speak to our college graduating class.

My love for design, color, and organizing "things" together has been with me since I was able to speak. My mother told the story of my five-year-old self that asked, "What we were eating for dinner the following week?" to my husband this last year. He chuckled at yet another piece of evidence that described me and my organizational tendencies.

I officially opened my design business doors in 2016, but was volunteering my time and talents for many years previous for church activities, Rodeo programs, school flyers, birthday cards, community events, and so on.

At a dinner with the incredible Shelly Yorgesen in 2017, I was rounding up my munchkins while my husband was speaking to her about her online business world. He mentioned the need for her design work could be fulfilled by myself. She reached out shortly thereafter, and we started working together on her online networking group. Over time, as I got better with fulfilling her needs on the design side, and as her business grew, I helped more and more on the administration and running of events.

A few years into the online networking business with Shelly, I find myself on a networking team hosting an event I helped plan and design graphics for! I was rubbing shoulders and spending meals with ladies and gentlemen who didn't pride themselves over the young entrepreneurs listening in on the advice and guidance that was given to the successful CEO's and executives in attendance.

Now, here I sit, next to one of the most brilliant men I know, and for the next twenty minutes, I am taught and asked to think only as Ron can do.

As I went about my duties for the next week of making sure diet restrictions were accounted for in the kitchen, guests were taken care of, forms were filled out, names were printed for lanyards, even to the lending of my own electrical converters. I was dubbed "event mom" by some of our fun and friendly guests as my ability to lead and guide were brought forward. I so enjoyed exercising my talents and getting to know this incredible group of men and women better.

Since my first conversation in the van with Ron, I made it a point to say hello every morning he came in for breakfast. As a hugger, I often embraced him in one and thanked him for his kindness and continual knowledge I was learning from him. One mid-morning, I was about doing my business, and was speaking with a guest when I felt a hand on my shoulder. There stood the ever warm and kind Ron, waiting for his morning hello.

Tears roll down my cheeks thinking of the effort and time he made to make me feel like someone in my position was important.

Ron and Caroline taught me so many valuable things that week. The simplest, in my opinion, had to do with simply looking into ourselves. He asked us what our spirit animal was. He asked what car we would be if we were one, what clothing brand we would be if we chose one, what color we are and so on.

Up to this point in my life, I hadn't ever asked myself these questions, let alone thought of them. I have always loved helping others feel comfortable, content and happy, and had realized I didn't take much care into doing it myself.   I knew who I was on the surface but didn't know who I truly was, deep down. I am so focused on others, I skip over myself—until then.

That night, after guidance of thought from Caroline for my spirit animal, I pulled my fuzzy socks on as I was getting ready for bed and got my confirmation. I noticed the animal we had spoken of possibly being, was printed all across my socks and then I realized it was all over gifts I had purchased for my daughters earlier that day. Not caring of the lateness of the hour, I excitedly texted Caroline a picture of my fuzzy socks along with the caption "I know what my spirit animal is,!" I was thrilled I had received my confirmation and was ready for the next step of my journey to me.

They started a spark that week. These incredible new connections and friends started me on a better path for myself. A path I plan to use for good in others' lives. I never planned or foresaw that a networking event with business owners and CEO's could give me such good friends and connections. Connections that would make me to be my best self.

I took this looking deeper concept home after our event to my husband and children, and we took time to figure out each other's sprit animals. How fun and humorous that was. Just this last week, completely out of the blue, one year after our 2019 event, my daughter drew me a picture of my spirit animal and our son sketched out my husband's animal. So precious how our kids can remind us of the parts of us that need to be urged continually forward.

My week at Crom Castle, may I say, was hardworking, educational and almost perfect. Just the way I wanted it. I absolutely loved learning from the many incredible men and women who came from different parts of the world to attend our ENE Symposium. These new "summer camp" connections that came from this week still influence me from all around the world, and I look forward to the future for all of us.

A special place is made in each of us, when we are blessed with a warm and welcoming opportunity of what we deem an incredible mentor or friend. But even more so when we are given the opportunity to return that chance to our new connections. I can't wait to be that spark in a new connections life, just as Ron and Caroline did for me.

JORDELLE LOVELL is the wife of a handsome Idaho farm boy and mother of her adorable two boys and two girls. She loves the country air with her horses and animals and keeps busy during the warmer months by working outside with her kids, attempting to teach them life skills and responsibility. Her favorite down time is sitting under a cozy blanket next to a fireplace watching *"White Christmas"* eating anything with chocolate or raspberries.

TOBIE SPEARS

Almost nine years ago, I was at a conference when one speaker mentioned she'd spent time living abroad in Guatemala. I sat in the audience and wondered where that country was located. I spoke with her after the conference and she gave me the contact information for the director of a private school in Guatemala. After emailing him, he offered me a position teaching English. So, my family and I rented out our home and after months of preparation, my husband Darrin and I loaded our daughters into our 2006 Ford Taurus and drove the 2780 miles to Guatemala from Utah. We spent twelve days exploring wonderful sights with our girls, who were five and nine years old at the time. We visited Lake Powell in Utah, The Grand Canyon in Arizona, Roswell and Carlsbad Caverns in New Mexico, and The Alamo in Texas.

As we were crossing the Mexican border, the border patrol

asked to completely empty our car so they could search it. We then spent the next few hours packing all our earthly belongings carefully back into the trunk. We spent several days driving through Mexico with the highlight being the night we excitedly ran into the ocean with all our clothes on in Veracruz. Each time the Federales stopped us to search our car they looked at us as if we were crazy. An American family with two young girls driving through Mexico with a teddy bear stuffed in the trunk.

When we crossed the border in Guatemala, we stopped at a market to purchase a cell phone and pay for minutes. We asked for directions and met the principal at the main mall, who asked us to follow her to our new house. Our home was 400 sq ft with the sink being outside in the backyard. We learned to wash all our dishes and clothing by hand and hang all our clothes out to line dry. For two months, I taught English while our girls attended classes on campus with me. Darrin did the shopping, housekeeping, washing and drying of all our laundry. Any chance he had, he would volunteer as a nurse with local doctors or mission groups.

On one such occasion, he spent the entire day volunteering at a clinic with a dynamic Guatemalan- American woman named DeAnn Ponciano. He'd told her about our family living nearby, and she invited us to spend a week at her lake house. She piled us into her van with her kids, her kids' friends, her neighbors, and her nephew, and we started our 8-hour road trip at 4:00 a.m. She opened her home to us and we had a glorious time exploring the lake, the magic of the river, and seeing new areas of Guatemala.

While at the lake house, DeAnn told the locals Darrin was putting together a medical clinic for anyone in need of medical attention and countless people came. Darrin led our group of volunteers as we worked for twelve straight hours helping anyone with any ailment. On our 8-hour car ride back to Guatemala City,

I peppered DeAnn with questions and scenarios of how to create a humanitarian tour for Individuals to experience life in a developing country. For twenty years, she had Guatemalan students traveling to the states to live with a host family, practice English, and have an American Thanksgiving, and I wanted to do what she has done in reverse.

Because of our time living in Guatemala, my family's eyes were opened to how hard life in a developing country was, and I wanted to share that experience with the world. Soon after our week at the lake house, our time in Guatemala came to a close, but my brain wouldn't stop. After we returned home, I invited DeAnn to spend a month living with us in Mexico as our Spanish teacher, and she also came to Utah to stay and visit our family. She has opened her heart and phone book to introduce me to her trusted drivers, Spanish teachers, Volcano guides, trusted friends, traditional Guatemalan cooks, clean and safe hotels, local NGO's she has worked with, schools and orphanages that are struggling, and much more.

Anytime I call DeAnn with a "big idea" she is up for the challenge. In November 2019 I asked DeAnn for the name of a school we could help.. In January 2020, my nonprofit had put together our largest fundraiser to date, and DeAnn put me in contact with the principal from a remote village whose elementary school has 200 students and 12 teachers. We decided we would supply every student and teacher with a brand-new backpack. They contained pounds of food such as beans, rice, pasta, peanut butter, sugar, hot tea, hot cereal, and a bottle of oil. We also included a pair of socks, a scarf, a hat, warm gloves, a jump rope, a toothbrush, toothpaste, and a big box of coco-rice cereal to top it off.

Days before my sister and I landed in Guatemala City DeAnn

had filled her entire garage with thousands of pounds of food and picked up 200 backpacks making sure she got us the best price. After we arrived DeAnn spent days driving us around to pick up the additional needed items. We filled her van multiple times and then spent days organizing and placing each item into all the backpacks and loading them into 3 vehicles.

We left her home in the pitch black before 5:00 a.m. so we could make the 2-hour drive and arrive on time to distribute all the backpacks. I planned for us to arrive two hours early, so we had time to organize the items before the students and their families arrived. To our surprise, as we pulled into the school, we saw hundreds of children and their families waiting in lines for us. When I asked DeAnn why they were all so early, especially since being on time isn't frequent in Guatemala, I was told they'd never been given the opportunity of such a gift. They wanted to make sure they didn't miss it. DeAnn spent the day helping us unload boxes from the vehicles, sort items, and translate for our group.

Whenever I ask, DeAnn has a referral for me. Whenever I need it, she's got advice and a willingness to help. In July 2020, I told DeAnn I was starting a free breakfast initiative for children in a remote village near Lake Atitlan. She has willingly helped with the logistics, ideas, and connections for us to be feeding and connections for us to provide 480 meals a month for 20 children who would not be eating breakfast otherwise. children who would not be eating breakfast otherwise. I've been leading humanitarian trips for the last seven years, and without a doubt, my nonprofit would not be where we are if it wasn't for DeAnn. The people she's introduced me to have become dear friends, and a trusted team, and I wouldn't be able to lead my trips without the support she's offered me.

My family and I have slept in every bedroom in her home,

have eaten meals with her family, and enjoyed her back patio as though it were our home. She makes sure we always feel welcome and wanted. She has become the friend of a lifetime, and I am eternally grateful our paths crossed in a small remote village in Guatemala. My life has forever been changed.

TOBIE SPEARS graduated from the University of Utah with degrees in Sociology and Political Science and a Certificate in Criminology. She is lucky enough to have one awesome husband, two amazing daughters, and three crazy cats. Tobie fell in love with traveling when she was 17 and backpacked through Europe and drove from Utah to Canada with her two best friends. After college, she started traveling with her husband and daughters and in 2002 they spent 3 months backpacking through central Mexico. In 2013 they drove from Utah to Guatemala where they lived, worked, and volunteered for 3 months. Tobie stays busy working as a birth and postpartum doula and running her non- profit organization *Guatemalan Humanitarian Tours* where she leads 11-day tours exploring the country, giving back, and having a blast while learning about life and how others live.

KELLY VAN NELSON

You Only Live Twice

It started with an impromptu encounter with MI5. Me, dressed to impress in a figure-hugging black gown, mingling at a corporate networking dinner in Edinburgh, trying to hide the fact imposter syndrome consumed me faster than an airborne virus. Unsuccessfully attempting to stop my shaking fingers from fiddling with the napkin as the swirl of people around me talked business.

I'd been allocated a seat at the best table in the house. My boss, a man who was a self-made millionaire and CEO of a large recruitment firm in the UK. The privilege of sitting with the 'Big Wigs' at the top table was permitted on two accounts. First, I'd been hurtling along in pole position as a top salesperson for some time, managing a complex portfolio of clients across Scotland, North East England, and Northern Ireland. Second, this was also my leaving party. Some irony lay in the fact my golden invite to the networking event of the year came just as I no longer cared about rubbing shoulders with the corporate crème de la crème. I'd just handed in my notice to leave the pinstripe suit on its hanger for a while, to head to South Africa with my husband. It was time. My sanity needed to spend quality time with my six-month-old daughter and two-year-old son.

"You're going to miss this," my boss said, nodding towards the lectern.

The cropped gray-haired lady who'd just evacuated the seat across the table from me was up there adjusting the microphone.

"I know I will," I replied truthfully.

"You sure there's nothing we can do to change your mind?"

"Not a thing."

I smiled and turned back to focus on the keynote speaker on stage. She was reminiscing about the time she was supposed to be picking up an informer to transport him out of the country, ideally alive. His cover had been bust wide open, and it was her job to get him to a small hanger where he would board an aircraft to fly him to safety. Only there was a snag. Her nanny had just called in a panic to say one of her daughters had taken seriously ill and been rushed to hospital. It was a matter of life and death. The anecdotes she shared of the situation unraveling enthralled me. How it was essential she kept a cool head, but not at the expense of losing her warm heart. The way she had to steady her breathing and think simultaneously of both her family and the man whose survival she had been entrusted to protect. In the end, through calmly weighing up her options, the perfect solution had appeared with clarity. She took the informant with her on a detour to the hospital, before ushering him along to his undercover departure lounge.

After her excellent speech, the elegant woman sat back down at my round table. Desperate to speak to her, I waited until dessert, then when the person next to her nipped off to the bathroom, I played a bold game of musical chairs and parked myself to her right-hand side. We spent some time chatting about the classic conundrum of balancing motherhood and working fulltime. I shared my plans to spend time in Africa with my family, children, and in-laws. She gave me insights into the highs and lows of being a counter-intelligence analyst and operative during the cold war espionage era. I opened up about needing to take a breather from the ongoing madness and pressure of the corporate world. We ate chicken wrapped in prosciutto and sipped Bailey's on ice.

I cite the meeting of this lady as the highlight of my early career and the reason I have become the sound businesswoman I am today. Always working hard at 100%, but never compromising needing quality time to be a wife and mum, nor ever giving up my side hustle of being a #1 bestselling author. The inspirational speaker was Dame Stella Rimington, Ex-Director General of MI5. The first and only woman to hold the top position in Her Majesty's domestic security service. I took home a copy of her autobiography, signed to my husband with a personal note on the opening page:

"You only live twice."

* * *

I started a new life in Cape Town after that meeting. One void of boardroom debates and sales targets. Filled instead with vibrancy and cultural diversity, of confronting moments embracing contrasts between poverty and wealth, gaining first-hand exposure to apartheid's complex politics of black and white. South Africa caught me by surprise, teaching me more than I could ever have learned about life and death, violence and peace, segregation and unity. This was more than I ever could have gained while sitting behind my desk in the icy-cold temperatures of Scotland. My love affair hugging vivid existence tightly to my chest while standing at the foot of Table Mountain lasted three years, and I will never be sorry.

Then we hit a bad patch. Violent crime was on the increase. The economy took a downturn and our small property portfolio took a hit. The children were moving into primary school years. It was time for a change. We weighed up the pros and cons of another major move to a continent neither of us had ever set foot in. At the end of that same month, we uprooted. Packed up the shipping container off the back of an employment opportunity I had quickly sought out, beckoning in Australia. An old business acquaintance of mine who I hadn't seen for several years took my call, and I shared with her my plans to leave South Africa and get back into recruitment. She needed someone experienced to help grow a newly established office in the red dust of Perth. The stars were aligned, but the job offer that followed was ultimately the result of adopting a diligent approach to building and maintaining a global network.

At the time of this upheaval, my husband was running his own business, so we rapidly pulled out all the stops to get our affairs into order. It was challenging, but there was nothing stopping us from taking the plunge. I'm lucky my husband and children share the same philosophy I do. We assess a situation and are open to taking calculated risks. Life is for living and embracing everything it brings with fearless zest and a sense of adventure.

* * *

Entering the business community in a new country as vast as Australia was daunting. The acquaintance from my Scottish days was now my new boss, but she lived on the east coast while I was settling into Perth life on the west. Aside from her, I didn't know a soul. Nevertheless, I threw myself into my work. I attended every industry event I could wangle an invitation to, following up with anyone I met with a connection request or message. And I reached out to contacts that might have a mutual reason to find common ground in business. I lost count of the number of coffee meetings I had every week. My tribe grew and Grew and GREW.

Networking is about respect. Greeting people with a smile and a firm handshake. Asking questions about them and listening to their response with genuine interest. Giving something first before you ask for something back and delivering on your promise. It's about jumping into that spare seat when there's someone you badly want to meet and the opportunity presents itself.

Simple.

* * *

I learned so much from listening to Dame Stella. This short but unique interaction helped me develop an inner confidence. Fueled me with the willpower to dig deep to find solutions to problems when the going gets tough. Armed me with self-belief that the underdog can make a difference. She said she could read people in the room by the kind of watch adorning their wrist. By the way the man in the crooked bowtie glanced with a bucketload of lust, and only a hint of guilt, towards the woman in vintage Gucci sitting three tables away because he still wore a wedding band. Or the new leather smell of the wallet containing a recently appointed CEO's embossed business cards that was assuring him of success.

In that one dinner, I learned more about the art of body language than the average person could in a lifetime. The former Director of MI5 read me and I read her. And I figured out the one white lie she told.

She did not tell the whole truth and nothing but the truth. You don't only live twice. You live every day that you wake up in the morning and chase your dreams with everything you've got, because only then will you make them a reality.

KELLY VAN NELSON is a bestselling author and poet from Newcastle-upon-Tyne, now living in Australia. Her poems, short stories, and articles have featured in numerous international publications and she regularly appears on radio and television discussing current issues prevalent in society. She is represented by *The Newman Agency*. *Graffiti Lane*, her powerful debut poetry collection, showcased at the London Book Fair and became an instant bestseller, raising awareness and influencing change around bullying, domestic violence, mental health, and suicide. Her books are frequently gifted to television celebrities, music icons, and Hollywood Oscar nominees and winners. Her second poetry book, *Punch and Judy*, is a #1 bestseller, shining a spotlight on turbulent love and domestic violence. Kelly is the recipient of a KSP First Edition Fellowship, an AusMumpreneur 'Big Idea - Changing the World' Gold Award winner for her creative use of the literary word as an antibullying advocate, a double Roar Success Award winner for Best Book (*Graffiti Lane*) and Most Powerful Influencer. She is also a 2020 Telstra Businesswoman Award Finalist and CEO Magazine Managing Director of the Year finalist. Kelly is also the mum of two children, wife of her soulmate of more than two decades and Managing Director on the executive board of a Fortune 500. In the spare time that she doesn't have, you can find her hanging out on the open mic performing poetry. In short, she is a juggler - **www.kellyvannelson.com**.

RYAN MC CLUSKEY & CATHAL BEACOM

Starting a business is a daunting task.

Little did I know the lightning bolt moment happened during a networking GAA (Gaelic Sports) sporting conference during Christmas 2017.

As I sat listening to the various speakers that Saturday afternoon, a multitude of questions entered my head.

I knew my playing days were ending; I had a young family, and I was in a job which provided little in the way of security.

'What am I doing at this event?'

'What am I going to do when I stop playing football?'

'Where am I in life? What does the future hold and what do I now want to achieve?'

These were the things that were swimming around my head that day. Then one speaker, who shared similar family experiences as me, talked about his jump into business. It wasn't this awe-inspiring speech or anything like that, but it resonated with me.

"I'm going to f**king do it and open a business because then at least I can say I tried," he said.

It was simple, and for some reason, these words stayed in my head.

I made my mind up from that moment that I was going to open my own business. At least I, too, could say I tried. As a member of the Gaelic Players' Association, (GPA) I was entitled to business networking help, so I went down that path. And so my journey towards opening my own business began.

In June 2018, the doors opened in Focus Recovery.

The aim of Focus Recovery was to deliver a sports recovery service, the first of its kind in Enniskillen, my hometown. For many years, myself and other sports people from my area needed to travel 30 plus miles to avail of such services. There was an opening for this type (or kind or sort) of product, and with this in mind, the company was formed.

Networking with friends once again proved essential in the basic et-upof the business. We pulled favors to get the show on the road, and with the Business Networking Scheme from the GPA, I could avail of the help that was on offer.

This scheme played a massive part in the foundation of my business. It also led to the establishment of many mutually beneficial relationships with other business people who also played in my sport.

It is probably only now as I write this that I realize these first steps through this networking scheme helped create and shape the business.

'Was the business unique?' 'Would the business be profitable?' These were questions I asked myself.

My business knowledge was pretty limited, so I quickly sought help through the local council, utilizing their 'Go For It' programme. This was a crash course in business for beginners. It explained all the basics to run a company and resulted in the formulation of the start-up business plan.

Starting good relationships, primarily through sport, with several business owners and gaining local contacts through the council programme has proven very important. From understanding the basic principles of the working environment to how poor networking systems in a business can lead to inefficiencies and failure, it was all vital. Even learning about business strategies, these are all valuable lessons gained in these networking processes.

Importance of business networking at the workplace

Business networking created awareness about the needs of all in the business, especially when I started.

Networking provided me with the skills of working with, and through people to achieve goals. Opportunities in my business were then identified by working with these other people from several business sectors. Such opportunities and help allowed me to further my company's work by approaching a close friend to come on board as a full business partner.

In under a year, the business, now called simply 'Focus', had taken the next step and delvedinto the health and fitness industry by hiring out a local football gym.

Connections through my local Gaelic football club aided this addition to the business, and it's through this networking advice that I identified important and profitable business improvements in the market.

Adding my close friend to the organization allowed the

business to identify potential business links and create a new customer base. The leap into this industry proved successful, and within weeks as we were outgrowing the small gym space we'd acquired.

By the start of year two, we decided to move to a bigger premise, one that could house all our services under one roof. We were on the move again.

As our business has grown in such a short period of time, we are continually networking and seeking as much help and guidance to pursue our business journey. Attending the Executive Networking Event (ENE) in Crom Castle in 2019 has helped us realize there are even more avenues for us to pursue in the health and fitness industry.

We can't claim these ideas, the power of communication and listening to others can. We have always believed in our business that if you close the book of learning, then you may close the book of business. With this in mind, the week-long event allowed us to communicate with many global individuals from a range of different businesses.

Truth be told, we felt completely out of our depth sitting with hugely successful business people who, financially, were on a different level to us. But, were we fazed being at the event? The simple answer was no.

No matter who you are or where you or from, business in any field throws up the same issues. The hurdles are predominantly the same in most industries, with different heights and widths. Ultimately, you still have to get over or around them. Listening to these people throughout the various days and activities gave us some brilliant insight into how to push our business to the next level. And as highly competitive and ambitious people, we intend to do so. Communication within any organization is effective, and one of the key components in running a successful business.

During the ENE week, we learned the true power of communication by exchanging many business ideas between and among several individuals.

As people communicated, we could create strong networks, and this was of great benefit to all the businesses in attendance.

We have made several new global friendships and remain in contact with these other businesses. It's amazing that in business setbacks and failure, if not communicated with the right people, can drive you deeper, sometimes into a world that is not real. People who are not in business give you advice, but they really don't understand. They don't know the dealings or the running of a business day to day. The ENE event gave us access to the right business mentoring people. Since the event, we still bash ideas on to the other business executives who were in attendance to seek help and guidance.

Communication is key. If you never ask the question, the answer will always be NO. Our advice to any business is to surround yourself with people in the know. Surrounding yourself with people who you know share in the love, respect, and the purity of an impossible search for the perfect business model.

As competition intensifies in the modern market, there is a need to come up with new concepts which capture the demand of the customers.

We can achieve this through communication and establishing good networks with the consumers. We are all for promoting ourselves through the power of social media, although we don't over elaborate on these platforms. We intend to let our actions to the talking and are currently building our structure and processes before we can start firing on all cylinders. If we get these correct, then our business can take on a new direction.

Look at any worldwide global brand, and the one thing they all have in common will be a solid business structure.

Conclusion

Hindsight is a wonderful thing. Everything that has happened in our business journey resulted from positive networking. We even got a chance to attend this once in a lifetime ENE event through networking with a client who we always confide in with business ideas.

Business networking is an important tool in the modern business environment. Effective communication and networking create business opportunities that can be identified through appropriate networks that can only help any business. Remember. if you don't ask, the answer will always be no.

RYAN MC CLUSKEY: I have worked in the sports and leisure industry for 15 + years. I started because of a desire for learning and improving my own sporting needs. I have developed an excellent overall knowledge of the health and fitness industry through my studies, obtaining a PGCE in secondary P.E teaching, a degree in Sports Science and the level 3 Personal Training Certification.

My area of expertise is working with sports persons & teams looking to improve their performance. With in-depth knowledge and experience of planning and periodisation of programmes, I help sports clients peak for competitions in their chosen field.

CATHAL BEACOM: Certified Personal Trainer with 8 years' experience. I got into Personal Training because I always enjoyed the gym and training. Playing sports at a high level, we always had strength and conditioning coaches in to push us to the next level. I loved the sessions so I went on to do my fitness instructing and personal training.

People think that fitness is a matter of looking good. To me it's about your health and mental wellbeing. You can then set yourself goals that can keep you on track and keep your mind positive.

The business of communication

From the second we are born we are communicating; we need to communicate to have our needs met even at one day old.

Communicating is a skill built throughout our life and develops as we grow and, dependent on environment and situations, we learn the skills to navigate communication.

Everyone can communicate, some people better than others, and people use different styles of communication. We communicate for different reasons in earlier years to have our needs met.

One valuable lesson I have learned in recent years is that

attending events and communicating needs to be as much about giving as receiving and communicating what we offer and what we need is equally important. Evidence suggests when you meet someone you know within seconds if you like them.

There is a part of the brain that activates when we meet people. It is called the rostromedial prefrontal cortex, or the do you like me/like me not part. We often connect quicker with people who are like us or have the same interests or that we perceive to have the same qualities as us. Like looking in the mirror, I suppose. It is easy to like and communicate well with these people, especially in a professional working capacity.

To really connect at a higher level takes more. A different part of our brain needs to be aroused and a feeling of connection needs to be present. This is the temporoparietal junction which becomes active when we share things with people such as a little about ourselves, our likes, dislikes, our dreams and some intimate things. This allows a higher frequency of connection and activates a high level of oxytocin, which is the neurotransmitter that enables us to bond and connect on a deeper level.

When in business, we can often become absorbed in business and use the business as a sole purpose to connect and only ever connect at that level. My experience has taught me that to achieve a real lasting connection you have to share: you need to know that what you have is worth sharing and your "why" is as important to share as explaining what you do.

I have worked in mental health for over twenty years and when at conferences, seminars or meetings, I would connect with lots of people, I am an extrovert, so I get my energy from people. I have great listening skills and like to talk myself. Interacting and building relationships comes easily to me with the right people. I do not say yes to every event, only those I feel I can offer something to and gain information or connections from. Social media is also a great platform for connections, though there is only so far you can build a connection on social media.

Back in 2018 I came across a post on social media about a tomorrow's leader opportunity. It immediately caught my eye as the caption was of women all different sizes dressed as Wonder Woman. I quickly clicked on the link and filled in my details. I live in a rural county in Ireland and opportunities do not come every day, so I decided I would have to go to them.

I received a response fairly quickly with more information to send in and a phone number of an event facilitator, Lisa Strutt. I phoned Lisa to discuss the program and the commitment and expectations expected. After a quick conversation, I decided this would be a good opportunity for me to expand my reach and circle.

Sometime later, I was contacted about our first event, a visit to the US consulate in Belfast. Looking forward to the event, I finished work early and made the two-hour trip to the city. Finding the time can be difficult as I work full time managing mental health services and I am also a co-founder of a charitable organization.

I did not know anyone, and after a few short introductions we went in to a large room and took a seat at the rather large table. I chose a seat in the middle of the table and drank a cup of tea. Just before we were receiving an address from the consulate, a lady came in and sat beside me. After a few moments we introduced ourselves, and to my delight and surprise it was Lisa Strutt, no coincidence I thought. Instantly we connected. There were many other events, one in Stormont and another in Dublin where we met up again and were allocated a mentor. My mentor was a lovely lady called Joanne who I learned a lot from and supported me with personal development.

Time passed, and Lisa and I kept in touch through social media. We nurtured and build a relationship.

Then something wonderful happened. My beautiful sister, Karen, and her ENE business partner, Shelly, were launching an executive networking event here in Ireland. I instantly knew I had to involve Lisa. Lisa is an expert in her field, and connecting people is very much a part of her many talents. We met in the city one day and discussed the event. Lisa was, as always, supportive of me and we set about supporting the event from our connections here in Ireland.

At the ENE event, I met many wonderful inspiring and thought-provoking people. My sister, Karen, has always been an inspiration and she, along with Shelly, brought together a castle full of like-minded business people and thought leaders. Ron Malhotra, who is a global leader outstanding in his field, attended and he's a very thought-provoking man. Understanding who you are and your why were both fundamental parts of Ron's message and one that I spent a lot of time considering.

These connections were complementing each other. I now had a "why," a story to share and other people as enthusiastic about taking action as I was. Lisa Strutt remaining an integral connection and our bond growing stronger.

It was then my business *"Mental Wealth International"* was born. I sought advice on registering the business, mentored through a business plan, received consultation and coaching by Lisa on *Mental Wealth International*, and this has been done through the power of connection in business. *Mental Wealth International* has grown from strength to strength supporting business to achieve mental wealth and wellbeing within their teams. They're coached through the process by Lisa Strutt and now part of the coaching circle that Lisa has developed.

Connecting is a great way of interacting with people learning and evolving as a person. I believe it is those real deep connections that stand the test of time and develop into much more, especially in business.

EMMA WEAVER is a member of the *Making Magic Happen Academy.* This is Emma's first book, one which came pouring out of her to reach out to people going through fertility challenges and treatment.

Her purpose in life is to advocate for appropriate support and services for those who need it within the mental health and wellbeing sector. She has over twenty20 year's' experience working in the mental health and wellbeing sector. Emma is the founder of mental wealth International and also works as a manager within Inspire wellbeing group.

Motivated by her purpose, Emma provides hope and support to others through both her professional and personal experiences. Emma currently resides in county Fermanagh, a beautiful rural county in Ireland. A, although a native of Clones, Emma lives very close to her homestead. She is the mother of mum to three beautiful children, who are her world and inspiration every day.

KAREN MC DERMOTT

There is nothing that I value more than the connections I have with people. I aim to be a positive in the life of others and I truly value others who are a positive in mine. I can share many stories of amazing connections, but the one I have chosen to share is the story about a turning point in my business.

In 2015, I had just had my sixth child, and I felt my home-based business was growing beautifully. I had been publishing for others for a few years at this stage, writing and publishing my own books, and was building good momentum. I strategically invested in my growth since my initial commitment of $50 per week. A seedling of an idea 2-3 years previously had grown, and my plan was to earn money publishing books for authors. I planned to reinvest it back into my business with the intention of building a million-dollar publishing press that I would sell. This would pay off my mortgage, and I'd live happily because I had the courage, vision and stamina to pursue a dream.

Right there in that moment, a miracle happened. It was the moment I set the intention to build Serenity Press into a million-dollar press.

Opportunities began to present themselves to me. One of which was that I had won a scholarship to attend the 2015 Ausmumpreneur conference. I was a mumpreneur who worked from home and didn't go to events or many things that took me away from my children. But I had set an intention I was committed too and I had a *Knowing* this opportunity was aligned with that.

So, with my four-week-old baby on my hip, I booked a room in the hotel the conference was in. I hopped on the red-eye plane to Melbourne, not knowing what to expect, but instead surrendering to the conference. If I was going to go, I was going to give it my all.

I was up for a Business Excellence award, which was a judged category, and so I made sure I was there for that. I went in but had no experience being judged for an award, and it was a learning experience. I didn't expect to win as it was all about figures and all I had at that point was a strong intention and not much money in my bank account.

The big thing that I didn't realize I would take away from this event was the connections I made. I had found my people, and it was the best feeling ever! These women genuinely were interested in what I was building; there was no competitiveness, just genuine support and recommendations. I remember sitting in the convention hall surrounded by hundreds of other mums in business from start-ups to million-dollar businesses. I had found my tribe. Two amazing women who fuel everything they do with grace and intention that every person in the room sees their true potential led this community. They worked really hard to pull off an amazing event with speakers who elevated everyone in the room on some level. Peace Mitchell and Katy Garner didn't put themselves on a pedestal, they hung out alongside everyone. When I spoke to them, they made me feel like part of their family. Being a business owner and event organizer, I know a million things would have been going on behind the scenes that needed addressing and yet they stopped and listened to me and gifted me time.

I remember sitting in the room and listening to the MC who happened to be Hay House author Susan Pearse, and I was thinking *It would be an absolute dream to be speaking to this room of women one day.* It was such a powerful moment, and I actually visualized it happening. It was a room that accommodated dreams and I believed with all of my heart that where there is a will there is always a way. So, I left that seed planted until I needed to take action.

When I got home from that conference, I was a changed person. The people I met, the connections I made, the knowledge I consumed all led to one thing, I needed to do biz bigger. I was playing the small game, and that is ok if I wanted to play the small game, but I didn't. I had set an intention to build a million-dollar business. It was then that I transitioned Serenity Press into a Traditional publishing house and founded Making Magic Happen Press where I could still assist first-time authors. Even on a personal note, I stopped waiting and started taking action. I hadn't been home in Ireland for seven years. I hadn't seen my sisters or stepped on Irish soil for seven years since emigrating to Australia. They had not met my four girls that I birthed in Australia, so I set an intention to take action. When Qantas announced a flight sale, I jumped on and grabbed me and my five kids who were living with me at the time, (my first son was eighteen and in Ireland for a gap year) and for $5000 AUD, I had return flights booked for us. If hubby could join us, he could grab a ticket later on. Everything felt aligned and moving forward.

I decided to mix business with pleasure and whilst in Ireland, I booked in a meeting with an Earl who so happened to own a castle I grew up visiting. I visualized hosting a writer retreat there and in that meeting it so happened that the castle owner and myself had aligned values and we put the wheels in motion. I booked the castle and started promoting it. Suddenly everyone was talking about Serenity Press and we signed an amazing author called Kate Forsyth, and the trajectory of our publishing press started to truly elevate. I felt a huge shift, and we pivoted well to maximize the potential to elevate.

I was all in and so when an opportunity came to share my publishing expertise in the Ausmumpreneur network and position myself as a publishing expert; I knew I had to make it happen, and I did. That led me to being asked to speak at the 2016 conference, and I also was an MC for the room. When I thought back to the thought I'd had in the room one year previously when my business was just a shadow of what it had evolved into in just one year, I smiled so much. This didn't feel like work, it felt like I was on the path to something genuinely great; I felt truly aligned with my highest potential. I also won my first business award at this conference, and a picture of me in a green dress was everywhere. I even had a full-page feature in the business section of an Irish newspaper. I felt like I had achieved it all, and yet it was another stepping stone on my journey.

Fast forward four years and I now own four publishing companies and a publishing academy. I have hosted four more retreats and worked with the most amazing human in Shelly Yorgesen to found ENE and pull off a next level executive retreat at the very castle I hired in 2016. This book has origins in this executive retreat as I worked with many of the contributors there.

I now have the honor of being the publisher for Sarah, Duchess of York and we have a 22-book deal for Serenity Press that we are working through, and that is bring huge opportunities for growth our way. KMD Books, which is my thought leader publishing press, is also publishing next level leaders, and MMH Press is where I publish my books and other books with soul essence.

My intention was set to build a million-dollar press, and I have achieved that, but I don't have plans to sell it yet. The journey is still too fulfilling for me to walk away. I love that I am now deemed to be an integral business woman who inspires others on their journey. To think that just by being ambitiously me, I lead the way for others is an amazing privilege that I will never take for granted. My advice to anyone starting out is to align with your values, find your purpose, learn what you need to and commit to growing.

Many people have just been through the toughest business year ever. 2020 has shaken the world and yet my business has thrived and that is because I have a model that works in any environment and truly amazing connections.

KAREN MC DERMOTT: Award winning publisher, author and advanced Law of Attraction practitioner, Karen McDermott, is a sought-after speaker who shares her knowledge and wisdom on building publishing empires, establishing yourself as a successful author-publisher and book writing.

Having built a highly successful publishing business from scratch, signing major authors, writing over 30 books and establishing her own credible brand in the market, Karen has developed strategies and techniques based on tapping into the power of knowing to create your dreams. Karen is a gifted teacher who inspires others to make magic happen in their lives through utilising her power of knowing strategies. She mentors multiple new authors through her *Everything Publishing Academy.*

After working with Karen, you'll walk away with essential tools and know-how to write and sell your book, get published or build your own successful publishing business, all in your own way.

Find Karen here:
www.kmdbooks.com
www.mmhpress.com
www.serenitypress.org
www.everythingpublishingacademy.com

SARAH BLAKE

The business of peace-making is all about connections. Broken connections, rebuilding connections, ending connections or even discovering new connections. Connection has been at the heart of what I do and not only do I understand it, but I apply it, live it and encourage it.

Not surprisingly, at its core, business is all about people and our ability to effectively work together. We need people if we want to grow our business. We need people to invest and spend their money on our business and we need our people to work together to achieve growth outcomes.

Have you ever had a business relationship sour? When it turns from something great into something that costs time, money and lots of energy to deal with? Perhaps it has damaged your reputation, cost you clients, or even lost you contracts? These are the reasons we need to make sure the connections we create are solid, based on shared understanding and trust. Because I often see the impact of when connections go wrong, I am conscious of how powerful it can be when we authentically connect with people.

When I reflect on the impact of connections on my own business, I have discovered something pretty interesting. Each time I have made the decision to take my business to the next level, it has been my connections which have provided the opportunity to pivot and shift. This isn't a passive thing. In fact, it takes focus and commitment to nurture relationships that are authentic, real and deep. It is worth it though, as our global world becomes more interconnected.

Every time I travel overseas, I make the effort to connect with the local mediation industry. I started doing this back in 2000 and continue to reap the benefits of some amazing diverse connections from across the globe. I am incredibly grateful that I get to call so many of these people friends, not just colleagues.

During a recent holiday to Singapore in June 2019, I made time to reach out and connect with the Singapore International Mediation Centre. I met some inspiring colleagues and share our experiences and challenges working in conflict across borders. The experience is a great example of how connections help you propel your business to the next level.

It's funny how small the world is, but one woman whom I met knew another colleague whom I met back in 2015 at a conference in Berlin and who now lives in South Korea. But that wasn't why we connected. It was more organic than that. We just shared an understanding and ease in our communication. We had shared experiences and were both passionate about training and empowering others.

I am incredibly grateful for this connection, because it

resulted in me receiving an invitation to attend the signing of the International Mediation Convention in Singapore in August 2019. I was also provided with the opportunity to pay it forward, which enabled a talented registrar to also attend the event with me.

Participating in this event provided an opportunity to really consolidate and grow my global connections. However, it wasn't until I sat in the room, joined by 1000s of fellow peace-makers, that I realized the significance of this opportunity.

A gathering of some of the most experienced, knowledgeable and passionate mediators and lawyers from across the globe. And I was right there in the mix. Speaking in front of some of my most inspiring colleagues and creating friends that I know will stand the test of time.

How has this translated to an opportunity to pivot my business? What has been the benefit? Whilst I don't usually track and measure these investments, it highlights how connections translate to tangible benefits. Within two weeks of attending this event, I was advised I'd been ranked in the top three of most searched for mediations in the International Mediation Institute's database. I have also had the opportunity to be appointed to the newly established Benchmark International Mediation Centre, China. Furthermore, my global connections and alliances have significantly expanded and I continue to build some opportunities that will transform my business.

Indirectly, but nevertheless part of the continuing story has been my recent acceptance of the ENE International Innovator of the Year award, which was presented in Northern Ireland. And wonderfully, one of my new friends from this adventure assisted in confirmation of my China connection. Such a small world!

Since I took the time to establish connections in Singapore, I have spoken at two international events. One of which was at Crom Castle, and I am currently negotiating terms for appointment on two other international mediation groups. The flow-on impact continues to profoundly affect how I think about the relationship of my business with the Asian market.

This is not good luck, nor is it the product of hard commercial sell. These opportunities are the direct result of me taking the time to invest in authentic relationships. To create connections with people that are real, honest and open.

Understanding these simple tips about making authentic connections may just help you take your business to the next level.

Stay true to yourself
the second you try the hard sell people instinctively react.
Push yourself out of your comfort zone
this is where the unexpected happens.
Follow up, give back
lasting relationship are based on reciprocity, respect and effort.

The relationships which I have fostered globally have been open and authentic. The drive has always been and remains curiosity and generosity, for how can your connections mean anything if you yourself aren't willing to come with an open heart. Whether we are conscious of this, we instinctively react to connections and assess their alignment to our own values. It isn't a matter of strategic opportunity, rather the authenticity is what drives the deep, lasting connections. This is where the magic and opportunity emerge.

SARAH BLAKE: *Multi Award-winning Mediator – Regional Business Awards 2018, Winner of Resolution Institutes Michael Klug Award 2018 and Young Mediator of the Year Award, Australian Disputes Centre 2016*

With more than 20 years' practice experience, Sarah understands the complexities of conflict and recognizes the high cost impact on business, community and individuals when resolution isn't achieved.

THE COUNTESS OF ERNE

My husband and I find ourselves in a rather unique situation in that our business is our home and our home is our business. We are incredibly privileged to live in Crom Castle, which is the ancestral seat of the Earls of Erne, my husband being the 7th Earl of Erne. The Victorian castle is set within a 1900-acre estate which is situated on the shores of Lough Erne in Co Fermanagh, Northern Ireland.

My husband's ancestors, the Crichton family, came to the lands of Crom from East Lothian in Scotland as part of the Ulster Plantation era in the early 17th century and have been here ever since. The castle in which we reside is not the original castle; the previous castle, having successfully withstood two Jacobite rebellions, was accidentally burned to the ground in 1764 by a careless maid. The 3rd Earl of Erne, my husband's Great, Great,

Great Grandfather, decided in the early 19th century to undertake the enormous task of building a new castle. He engaged the services of the noted architect, Edmund Blore (most famous for his design of Buckingham Palace, but also responsible for Lambeth Palace, Government House in Sydney and Voronstov Palace in Crimea). The building of the new castle was not without complications, when near to completion, a further fire caused considerable damage and elements had to be reconstructed. The present castle was eventually completed in 1841.

It is rare in the 21st century to find a stately home within the British Isles that is not in some sense commercial as families have dealt with taxes, divorces, death duties and the mistakes of previous generations. At the beginning of the 20th century, there were a series of Land Acts in Ireland which led to the splitting of large estates to less than 2,000 acres. The Crom estate, which now stands at 1,900 acres, could certainly not be considered as a modest landholding, however, the land is not fertile and has little farming value. The poor quality of land meant the estate was unable to support the running of the house, and with the onset of the well documented 'Troubles', finances became a serious concern. Because of the political situation and instability in the region, commercial ventures were largely not viable.

Thankfully for Crom, in the 1980s, the National Trust were looking to take on further properties in Northern Ireland with a particular interest in gaining land. The Crom Estate is one of the most important nature conservation areas in the United Kingdom, and there is a plethora of flora and fauna to explore. In addition to the wonderful wildlife present, it is an area of outstanding natural beauty; the landscape having been designed by Gilpin. Lough Erne weaves through the land and together with the two inland lakes, there a sense of being surrounded by water and the subsequent light effect can be extraordinary, particularly with the ever-changeable Irish weather. In 1988, the National Trust took over the running of the Estate and all the estate buildings, including some twenty-one of which are listed. The Trust continues to run the estate today, which is open to visitors, but the castle and surrounding gardens remain in our private ownership.

Prior to the death of my Father-in-law, my husband, then Viscount Crichton, lived and worked in London as a real estate buying agent. It was in London in 2012 that we met one evening at a dinner party, neither of us probably realizing how important that encounter would subsequently be. Life changed abruptly for John, my husband, on 23rd December 2015 when his father died at home at Crom, and as a result, he became the 7th Earl. It was time to pack up his company in London to return home to Ireland on a permanent basis as custodian of this beautiful castle. Beautiful it is, but it is also 150,000 sq. foot of Victorian rooms and plumbing. The annual bills are far from inconsequential, and it would be unaffordable to live here as previous generations had with a full live-in staff (not quite Downton Abbey, but not far off). More-so, it would be impossible to live here at all. When you love something however, you are prepared to go to the ends of the earth to protect, to nurture and enhance it. Make no mistake, Crom Castle is loved. It is a much-loved center of a community. It is a loved place of work. And it is a loved as a historical, architectural treasure. It is loved for its landscape and its beauty. Most of all, it is loved as an extra-special family home.

It is a fine balancing act using your home commercially without changing the ethos of it. We have decided to make Crom available to rent either as an entire castle, or there is a separate smaller wing which you can take. The castle comes fully staffed with our cook, butler, housekeeper, etc. The idea is to invite people into our home, albeit as a paying guest, but as though you are our private guests. When you stay at Crom, you will be treated as a friend, you can wander freely from room to room. You can even plan with the cook what meals you want and make cocktails with the butler in the bar. You will see our family photographs sitting on top of the piano and you will hear the occasional bark from our (very friendly) dogs as they run off down the lawn in chase of something.

When the 3rd Earl commissioned this building over 200 years ago, it was not intended to be lived in all year round. In fact, it was intended as a sailing lodge which the family would come to for three months in the summer and perhaps for Christmas and Easter. It was built for entertaining; it was built for fun. So rather than opening the doors for tours to the public, or any number of other ventures which we could have explored, we would rather try to stay closer to what this building was intended for in an attempt to maintain its integrity. There are further perks to this concept for us also in that we both get to meet a variety of interesting people. We both consider ourselves to be people persons and love interacting with new people as well as old friends and family. It gives us huge pleasure to share our home with people and for them to build memories and relationships here.

My husband and I built our own relationship here on weekends when I would fly over from London. It is here that we got engaged and where we got married. Little did I know back in 2012 that sitting next to John at that dinner party would result in me moving to Ireland and entering the hospitality industry (whilst still working as an Art Advisor in London). We have both developed new skill sets and are very involved in all aspects of the running of the castle and events. Often, I have cooked the food we serve and I always pick and arrange the flowers. It is John who you will speak to on the telephone when arranging bookings and planning an event. We are incredibly hands on and thankfully, work extremely well together with the support of a fantastic team.

This is a business built on relationships. There is one relationship however that is absolutely key to this business. It is at the absolute core of it and the essence of it. It is the relationship that inspires and drives us daily. And it is the relationship which keeps us going and makes it worth it through blood, sweat and tears. It is our relationship with our home. Crom Castle is our business, it is our past, it is our present, it is our future. Crom is our home and we are here as custodians to ensure that it is here for the next generation, for their future. We are very lucky, and we want to share this unique place with special people and have some fun along the way.

THE COUNTESS OF ERNE:
Harriet was born and raised in the Scottish Borders, spending her childhood weekends and holidays with her brothers exploring the surrounding countryside. She went to school at St Leonards in St Andrews Scotland where she excelled in sport, drama and art, but both spelling and discipline were skills which alluded her.

Following school, she spent time in Florence, Italy, studying a diploma in art at the Charles Cecil Art School and the British Institute, where she studied Art History and Italian. Harriet obtained a degree in Art History from York University, and subsequently secured a job at Christie's auctioneers. Harriet continues her work in the art world in London and in Ireland as an art advisor at Hanover Art Advisory.

In 2019 Harriet married John Crichton, the 7th Earl of Erne, becoming The Countess of Erne. They live together with their dogs at Crom Castle which is situated in a 1900 acre estate on the shores of Lough Erne in Co Fermanagh, Northern Ireland. The Earl and Countess host a variety of events at this historic castle which is also now available for private hire.

LISA CROFTON

A Chance Encounter Leads to the Chance of a Lifetime

Sometimes a chance meeting is just that: two people in the same place at the same time for the same reason without any pre-planning. That's how it was with Melissa and me. Our children happened to be in the same stage play, which meant we took up nightly residency next to each other in the theater seats while they rehearsed.

Our friendship was easy and fun. I liked her immediately. She was one of those souls who feels authentically open, kind, and ready with a smile. One other thing drew me to her; she had a way of making you feel 'seen'. While she radiated with a natural beauty, she seemed unaware of her sparkling presence. Instead, she was focused on those around her; asking questions, expressing genuine interest and laughing from her heart. Perhaps that's why, when she told me of her ailing husband, her tone was void of complaint or self-pity.

Jay was ill with throat cancer for the second time in their short life together. This time was much more serious and the prognosis, despite their valiant effort to fight it, was inevitable. With their busy contracting company to run and two little girls to raise, Melissa faced the truth with bravery and resolution. I was awe-struck by her composure.

So, when I received word that Jay lost his battle, I took to my pen and what I do best: expressed my sympathy to my new dear friend in written sentiment. My words intended to convey my deep understanding of her pain underneath her bravado.

Having just experienced a series of painful losses myself, it was easy to relate. After returning home from vacation, I discovered a heart-warming message on my answering machine from Melissa thanking me for my words and suggesting I should be writing greeting cards. I had a good chuckle and felt pleased with myself.

It might have stayed there, but during that same round of messages, another friend was thanking me for her birthday card sentiment. I had a habit of rewriting store-bought cards, never feeling they captured my feelings accurately. Before the recording ended, she said, "You should be writing greeting cards."

There is a feeling you get when the right seed is planted in your creative brain. It's the same feeling you get when you lock in that last puzzle piece or debut a masterful gourmet dish. You are equally stunned and satisfied at its solidifying path. I'd been searching for a way to use my gift of words while I was recovering from my own grief. Upon hearing the same phrase uttered from two people I adored, that feeling set in.

I sat down one day and channeled all my grief into messages from the deepest recesses of my soul: about friendship, family, loss, celebration, support, connection and love. Seventy-two messages in all. I felt as though I'd poured all my grief, wisdom, love and joy into those little paragraphs. It felt amazing. I was certain they were worthy of the publishing community. I sent them promptly to all the major greeting card companies for possible publishing. All the major greeting card companies promptly sent them back with a final 'no thank you'.

At first, I was disappointed and was ready to tuck them away for good. But something kept pushing me to keep going. I went back to my drawing board (my kitchen table) and set out to design my own greeting cards. Just because the big dogs didn't want them, that didn't mean the bones weren't good.

I added my own artwork and printed the verse on my 'run of the mill' laser jet printer. By the time I was done, I had created a unique self-closing card design with no-two-the-same art designs. I was ready for market. I used my experience in direct sales to create at home parties where I sold my cards in theme packs, gift boxes and a single serve option. Melissa was my first hostess. She called herself 'my biggest fan'.

After a year of two to three home shows a week where I nearly sold out every time, recreating the inventory was becoming almost impossible. It was not unusual for me to sell 200-250 cards in one show. I often held card-creating parties on the weekends: I put family, friends and neighbors to work cutting, folding, printing and sponging. Sponging was the finishing touch on my unique hand-painted designs. But people are only willing to volunteer for so long. I had finally come to a crossroads: go big or go home.

I was in church one Sunday morning and I put my dilemma

to spirit. I remember feeling very small and thinking, "I just don't know which way to go, quit or expand? And if I were to expand, how?" I finally conceded to the universe: if it is to be, show me how to make it happen. As fate would have it, Melissa was also part of that small church community.

Directly after that service, as church members shared coffee and conversation, Melissa, unaware of my dilemma, approached me. She said, and I quote, "Are you ready to take your greetings cards to the next level?"

I still remember the exact spot I was standing when I heard her question. Speechless, I'm not sure I responded. She continued, "My accountant says I made too much money last year and need to invest in something. I love your cards and think everyone should have access to them." That moment changed everything. Guess I was 'going BIG'.

'Going BIG' meant obtaining a U.S. patent on the unique die cut style, finding a die cutter that could handle the Victorian style edging and the special enclosure. Then hiring a sales representative, securing bar code numbers, placing the cards in the hand of a trustworthy fulfillment house and selecting a suitable display case for retailers. It was a whirlwind of marketing activity and I would not have enjoyed it without the constant support and reassurance of business- minded Melissa.

Before all was said and done, our card company 'Creative Versetility' had placed sentimental card collections in over sixty-five card shops along the East Coast and took us on unforgettable business and personal ventures.

Eventually, the dream of having my card verses recognized by a major card company manifested. Executives from Blue Mountain Arts, a global greeting card giant, viewed my work at an international stationery show where our companies were represented by the same group. Another chance meeting that resulted in an 8-year writing contract. Subsequently, my work was published in anthologies, inspirational calendars, greeting cards, and poetry books.

One of my sympathy verses was used as published card verse superimposed over an American Flag and signed by seven hundred employees sent to Barnes and Noble co-workers who survived the 9-11 attack in NYC. My Mother's Day sentiments were requested for availability by U.S. soldiers stationed in Germany. Two stand out moments in a stand out adventure.

My by-line was side by side with the likes of Rumi, Oprah Winfrey, Ralph Waldo Emerson, Elizabeth Kubler Ross, Confucius, Anne Morrow Lindbergh and many others. A mind-blowing experience for a young mother and aspiring writer. It was also the beginning of an expanded writing career. I would go on to write a newspaper column, a weekly feature article in a local paper, and take advantage of contributing authoring opportunities. All this, because of a chance meeting with someone who believed in my talent, my vision, and my professional future.

Sometimes a chance meeting is a just a chance meeting, and sometimes it is the first step in a lifelong dance between two souls meant to create something special. One chance meeting that led to a dynamic professional collaboration. A chance meeting that grew into a powerful partnership, friendship and unforgettable journey.

LISA M CROFTON: Master Life and Business Coach LMC Consulting & Mentoring, LLC Owner, The Positive Living Center, Author, Hope, Healing and The Way Forward

Speaker: Mastering Work/ Life through The Four Agreements Specializing in Organic Marketing, Coaching Development & Intuitive Intelligence

Lisacrofton.com
Lisacrofton88@gmail.com
860 637-2393

TANYA CROMWELL

How do you build a 25-year amazing career without having to make a single sale? Networking! Yep, that "thing" that everyone hates to do—Networking! I have a successful design company that designs and draws blueprints for over 125 houses per year and a construction company that builds Custom homes for amazing people. And I do not feel I have ever had to "make a sale" in the traditional sense. Yes, Networking gets a bad rep, people do not like to do it. So, for this article, let's not use the word networking, let's use relationships, because for me, it is all about building relationships.

Twenty-five years ago, I could not find a house plan that I liked, so I decided, ok, I will just draw my own. We built that home and it is where I raised my kids for almost twenty years. When I had a friend asked, 'Hey, can you design my home?' I said,

'Sure,' and from there, I found my passion. Who knew I would make a career out of it, let alone have the privilege of making people's dreams come true? So, I started learning and becoming more efficient at my skill while managing a retail furniture store. I decided I needed to be around construction more, so I joined a local Home Builders Association to be around people who knew more than I did. You know that adage about "be the dumbest one in the room so you have nowhere else to go but up?" Yes, that was me. I just wanted to learn from others who had made it and were successful.

I went to those meetings with a mindset of learning from others, and in return, I would give them service anyway I could. I volunteered for committees, boards, and leadership positions. I served in every capacity I could along the way, just to talk with people and glean their knowledge about building houses and being a successful designer and contractor. I even stepped up for six months and served as the local Executive officer for the Association while we were looking for a permanent candidate. I was the first Female Local President in Eastern Idaho, the first Female President in the State Association, and the first Female Builder Rep for the State of Idaho for the National Association. Was it a lot of time, hard work, boring meetings, and sacrifices? You bet it was, but I can honestly say I am where I am today because of the amazing relationships that I built along the way.

Today, I am proud of what I have accomplished, and I hope to help others build their careers and live their passions through mentoring and helping them along the way. There are a few pieces of advice I always give to people when they are starting a new career or trying to build their business. One of the first things I tell people to do is to surround yourself with amazing people who know more than you do. But you do not do this by asking, "Hey, will you be my mentor?" You do this by asking yourself, what can I do to help this person out? How can I serve them?

When I walk into a room and meet a new person, I find out as much about them as I can. I even try to take notes in my phone about them. Things like who their kids are, what is their spouse's name, what is their favorite food, etc. Then I figure out a way to serve that person. It may be someone who you think, *I have nothing to give that they would ever need*, but you must look for the opportunity to serve them. Let me give you an example. I was at a Legislative event once and talking with a builder. He mentioned that he liked golf. The night continued, and he said he was headed to Texas the next week. I excused myself and went to the ladies' room, called a friend who lived in the area where he was headed and asked where the best golf course was and if he had any connections with that course. When I went back into the event, I had a name and number to give this builder of a guy who would get him on a private course at a discounted rate. This builder was my competition. Why was I doing this for him? Well, let me tell you, I have learned more from this guy than any book or class could have ever taught me, and all it took was a simple phone call. We have been friends for many years now and I know I could call him and ask him for advice at any time. He was already a successful contractor and was someone who I looked up to. You know, one of the smart guys in the room! I served him, built a relationship, and he became my mentor without even knowing it. It may even surprise him when he reads this.

When I meet a potential client, I do the same thing. I do not treat them like I am trying to make a sale; I treat them like they are a friend that is starting something that they have no idea how to do. I teach them what they need to know. We sit down and they are so excited about drawing a new house plan or building their dream house, and we talk about their dreams. What they want, what they have done. I ask lots of questions. I give them advice about their property, where to go for banking, what types of loans there are, what the different stages of building are and how long it will take. I ask the questions that they never even knew they needed to ask. I do this all without expecting them to "be my client". I just want building to be a good experience for them. So, I tell them what to watch out for, I tell them how to check out their contractor to make sure they are a good fit, and so many other things. By the end of the meeting, I have not even talked about my company or what I do. They usually ask, "So will you please draw my plan?" without even asking what my prices are. I build that trust and relationship with them by giving away as much free advice as I can. If they build with me or with someone else, they leave my office with a good feeling and settled nerves, and what is my reward? Why do I do all of that? Referrals. I do not have to sell because my customers do it for me. If they know of someone building a house that needs plans, they gladly refer people to me. No sales, just relationships!

When you are creating your dream job, it is a lot of hard work, sacrifice and commitment. But make sure you are working on the right things. Work on helping others so you can learn from them, work on creating relationships with the right people in your industry. Work on teaching people what they do not know. Relationships, relationships, relationships! That is the reason I am where I am today and why I am living the best life I can live. It never feels like work when you get to make people's dreams come true.

TANYA CROMWELL has been designing and drawing house plans for 25 years and her firm designs over 125 homes a year as well as doing the Renderings for *The Parade of Homes* in Eastern Idaho. Her Design company uses 3D modeling as well as colored build plans for her clients she serves. Tanya also became a contractor 7 years ago and her company builds about 15 to 20 High end custom homes in the Eastern Idaho Area. Tanya Cromwell is currently serving as the National Rep for the State of Idaho at the National Association of Home Builders. She was the first female president for both Local and State Builders Association as well as the National Builder Rep and delegate for the state of Idaho. Tanya has received many awards over her career including Associate of the year and Builder of the Year. She has also received the 2019 International Builder of the Year Award from Executive Networking Events in Ireland. She also received Builder of the Year for the State of Idaho in 2019. Tanya also serves on 5 board of directors for various charities and is currently writing a book. In her spare time Tanya likes to golf, travel and volunteer for organizations that she is passionate about. She has coached Varsity level Fastpitch softball for about 15 years including Highschool and travel ball teams. Tanya has 3 adult children that are her biggest accomplishment and what she is most proud of.

Idaho Home Design / NEXT Construction Solutions
1798 Curtis Ave. Idaho Falls,
ID 83402 208.589.9558
tanya@idahohomedesign.com

DANI McFERRAN

Stepping off the underground at the former World Trade Center in New York City, I looked up at those enormous escalators stretching heavenward. I could hear the bustle of the city above. I was excited, nervous. I remember wondering what it must have felt like on that fateful morning over ten years ago on 9/11, for those workers making their daily commute into the heart of New York's beating financial heart. Did the day feel like just another? Did they still feel the buzz of coming to work in the epicenter that is The Big Apple as I was? I had read it had been one person's first day at work, and sadly, their last.

I felt both deliriously happy and nauseously petrified. I took a deep breath and boarded the escalator, moving skyward. The bolt of blue from that sky only a true New Yorker gets used to, caused me to smile ear to ear in anticipation to get out into that glorious sun-soaked metropolis. So many thoughts bounded in my head: would this office work out? Who was I to be opening a place in NYC just two years into starting my own design company? A girl just out of her 20s, with no funding, no financial help, hailing from a small town near Belfast, Northern Ireland - those girls just didn't do this sort of thing! It didn't seem real.

Much time had passed from my first visit to Manhattan, when the towers still featured as the defining architecture of New York's iconic skyline. I had just finished my studies at Savannah College for Art and Design. It was arguably the best Art School in the States, and one that George Lucas (of Star Wars fame) preferred for their incredibly high level of talent. I was returning home via New York and wanted to spend some time in the city of dreams before I left. Much of it was with friends at twilight picnics at the Triborough Bridge - a special place that offers the best views of the city and those two towers. Now I was here opening a second office, the first of mine outside of Ireland. Time moves on. Worlds change.

The journey to get me to the States was the first time I learned about the power of connection and just how it plays an integral piece of your life's journey of progression. Both at the time of it happening, and the ripple effect it has on the rest of your life.

I had moved to the North West of Ireland to study Graphic, Product & Interactive Design in Derry/Londonderry under Justin Magee, new to the role of Course Director coming straight from working at Porsche, Smart MCC and LEGO Systems. He was at the very top of his game. His passion for the craft of design was infectious. I was truly inspired to push past my boundaries of what I thought I might achieve and saw in him inspiration to move beyond Ireland in my design career. After a successful two years of study, I yearned to work with a company to further my skills and gain real industry experience, like Justin, before I finished my final year and graduate. Nothing had ever been done in the faculty's history to facilitate this so, naturally, I took it upon myself and create such a path - something that has become a common theme in my life.

We discussed the idea of me working and studying in the States; the University of Ulster had links to two Universities in Georgia and Alabama. I could study and work there with the companies the Universities had links with - Compaq/HP and GE Plastics. A proposal was put to the Dean, the Professors at the two Universities were approached and things were moving in the right direction. But we needed something that would demonstrate just how much this endeavor would mean for me personally, what is represented on the grander scale and for the University seeking to build international connections.

I was from a small town outside of Belfast, capital of Northern Ireland. A city steeped in political unrest. Forty years of The Troubles had ravaged shop faces, ruined businesses, and hardened hearts. Slowly, however, times were changing. Politicians were pushing for social change, acceptance of our differences to build a better future for ourselves and generations to come. The country as a whole yearning for growth and America, at that time, was very supportive and responsive to that cause.

The Irish, north and south, are a unique breed. We have endured the worst of hardships yet still offer world class hospitality. We greet the needy, the weary, the tired, the hungry - with open arms and an open heart. And we create connection in a room full of strangers - if you are lucky enough to have an Irish friend you will know this universal love and enjoy a very special bond.

A case needed to be made. A voice needed heard.

My Head of Department, Anton Hutton, knew the right

person. John Hume (sadly recently deceased) - was widely regarded as one of the most important figures in the recent political history of Ireland. He was one of the architects of the Northern Ireland Peace Process and was Nobel Peace Prize joint winner in 1998. He believed in connection. And he believed in creating new paths. Anton reached out, explained the scenario we faced and lo-and-behold, I received a personal letter of recommendation urging this unique relationship to be cultivated and for myself to carve out that path for a union of minds. It worked.

The program was a hit. Studying and working at SCAD and Auburn University changed my life. I was immersed in a design world that was totally global - the students, my professors, the companies I worked with, the projects I worked on. I learned there were no boundaries in design, or in design thinking. Professor Victor Emoli, now Dean of the School of Design, taught me how to connect my knowledge of the world and translate that into informed, successful brand design, product design and human-centered interfaces.

Fourteen years later, I sat at the mirror pool of Ground Zero, a short distance across from my new international office I was opening on Broadway. Here at this pool I thought about all the lives that had been lived and lost here. I looked into those waters and felt the ripples of John Hume's letter in my life. That connection - his endorsement and encouragement for me to go forth with curiosity and hope and forge a new chapter - brought me to a place where dreams are made and icons topple. Like Belfast, New York faced a major rebuild. Not just physically, but soulfully. What has since become the mantra of my company - Regroup, Reframe, Refocus - was what NYC lived through, and it galvanized.

As I started my first day at work looking out across that

skyscraper skyline, I smiled at just how far I'd come - this girl on her own from Belfast with the big dream. All those people brought together, the power of their connections. My worry faded, replaced with the thrill of living and working in the biggest of cities as I began to dream even bigger.

 **DANI MCFERRAN** is an award-winning, passionate and experienced creative innovator currently based in Belfast, NI; creative director to her design consultancy, *Done and Dusted Design*. With an international background in branding, product design and UX/UI, and over 14 years of working with industry leaders in a variety of markets, Dani's multi-faceted abilities and global edge has demonstrated a history of making a successful difference in the renowned design studios and world-ranking companies she has worked for and in. Guest lecturing in universities in the USA and NI, Dani is an enthusiastic advocate for women in tech and is working with the likes of Silicon Valley-funded start ups in the design and implementation of big data for beautifully designed apps.

SARAH FLYNN

"Any Questions?" said the voice at the front of the room. And I had lots - a captivating 20-minute talk from a power couple who'd built up an £8.6 million pound property portfolio in three years. Impressive, isn't it? I definitely thought so.

It was October 2019, and I was sitting in one of many property courses I'd signed up for to educate myself further as a property investor and take my business to the next level. The power couple I referred to–Nina and Richard Peutherer–had similarly undertaken the same course a few years previously. They'd learned about Houses of Multiple Occupation, and how to use this strategy in the UK Market to make a small fortune.

Their success story left me inspired, in awe, and blown away. They explained they would hang around at the back for fifteen minutes or so during the break for anyone to come and speak to them about their journey. I'd felt particularly drawn to Nina during the talk. So many things Nina mentioned, I found relatable. She'd suffered with a fear of public speaking, as did I, but she spoke with such confidence now and was clearly a strong, independent woman and a successful business owner. Nina has gone from shaking with a microphone at the back of a classroom to sharing a stage in LA with Vanilla Ice. She'd broken into the international property market. I wanted to break into the international property market. I felt I needed to introduce myself. Something told me there was an opportunity in it, though I was not exactly sure what it was at the time.

I waited until others had finished chatting with Nina and when I saw a gap; I walked over to strike up a conversation. Unsure what I really wanted to get out of the introduction, I began by explaining my wonderment for Nina's achievements. We spoke of some of my personal projects I currently had going on, and Nina seemed genuinely interested. At the end of our brief encounter, Nina said, "Find me on Facebook and let's keep in touch." And I did.

In the mist of this happening, like most budding entrepreneurs, I was reading numerous coaching books, which all seem to echo one another. One of the overriding commonalities of these hugely successful people was that they all had mentors. In the weeks that followed after meeting Nina, I pondered on the idea of Nina becoming my mentor. She seemed like the perfect fit. I contacted her on Facebook to ask if she'd consider having me as a mentee. Her response was thoughtful and considered, citing that she had been asked on many occasions to mentor others but has never taken up the offers because of work commitments. Her message ended that she would have a think on it and come back to me in the New Year.

I waited patiently for the New Year to arrive and sure enough, as promised, in early January 2020, Nina replied with her decision. My excitement was beyond belief when she agreed to coach me. I felt I was lucky, but also that fate brought us together, and that I'd taken the opportunity I saw in front of me a few months ago, even though back then, I did not know its purpose.

We scheduled our first session only a few weeks later and got work right away on expanding my business, studying property deals together, and raising my profile as a property expert and public speaker.

It's fair to say since that first session with Nina, my world has changed more than I ever could have imagined, and I have achieved things I never thought possible. First, I learned a lot about business, and though I'd been running a business for three years, it's profound how casting a fresh pair of eyes over it can change enhance it. Within the first two weeks, I had a new website, several new social media profiles and pages, new marketing strategies and made many changes to help protect my business long term.

The second, and probably most obvious thing given that we are both property investors, is we have worked together to expand my portfolio. She has analyzed countless deals with me to help me make better, faster decisions in property, which has enabled me to go onto to buy multiple properties at once.

Another enormous change for me has been network expansion. Nina has taught me the value of networking, and how to network with purpose. This change has been exponential, and led me to start my own podcast, which to date has been listened to in twelve different countries across five different continents. It has given me the opportunity to meet with and interview some exceptional individuals including Paralympic Gold medalists, world leading scientists, multi-million-pound business owners and film producers. Nina gave me the skills and confidence to join other high-level networking events. This opened the door to being asked to speak at events about my journey, liaise with multi-million-pound investors and even enabled me to feature in this anthology.

It's hard to believe how much my life has changed in eight short months. I've accomplished things I didn't know I had in me.

There's an entrepreneurial saying that it only takes one person, one connection, one opportunity to change the course of your life forever; and I am living proof of that. Imagine the hundreds of thousands of people you speak to in your life. Most of them will be relatively insignificant, and it may take years to meet that one person who can change your life. But imagine that when you meet that one person, that everything you ever wanted, all your hopes, dreams, desires, they all come true. That's the business of connection.

SARAH FLYNN is a successful Property Investor/ Developer and Business Owner, and has built up a portfolio using 2 main strategies of HMO's (House Shares) and flips. Sarah has invested heavily in the UK property market, and focuses on making multiple income streams out of each property as opposed to buying property in volume. Sarah started her career in the corporate banking world, spending almost 10 years in the financial sector, working for global giants *Lloyds Banking Group*. Previous positions included a number of sales operational roles, Risk and Audit Manager roles and high-level Project Management roles. Her company - *KAF Properties* - was founded in 2016, following the tragic death of her 19 year old brother, which had a profound impact on her life, leading her into pursuing her dream as a serial entrepreneur. Sarah regularly speaks publicly about her journey, in her mission to inspire others to also believe that there is life after trauma. Sarah' is also the owner and host of an inspirational podcast called *The Ambitious Entrepreneur* - where she interviews hugely successful people such a multi-million pound business owners, Olympic gold medallists, and film producers; discussing what continues to drive them forward, and what's made them as successful as they are today.

JAMES BILLMAN

The Story of Connection and an Ongoing Journey

My name is James Billman. I've been a business owner for over twenty-eight years. I have owned multiple businesses, starting with a catering company, which led into a production company, four steakhouses, a Real Estate Company and a few other businesses. I have seen the power of connection within every one of my businesses. The story of connection I would like to share with you is one that started out with a simple idea. It's based on watching my youngest daughter struggle in school at very young age until she recently found her confidence through riding her horse. I started thinking about her journey and her story and the potential impact it could have amongst other struggling individuals.

Through a business connection, I learned of a woman named Karen McDermott from Australia who was offering an opportunity to teach others how to write a book with step-by-step instruction. Upon signing up for the program, I shared my ideas with Karen and other business people. I learned from my businesses that I think out loud and share my business concepts as though I am already doing those concepts to see what their reactions are and to see if they approve. Based on other's reactions, I usually decide whether my concept is a sound concept. I like to see people's first reactions. Their reactions were almost overwhelming with support. I came up with the idea of the book and decided that this was something that our community, kids, and everybody could benefit from. I called it: "Cowboy Warrior Project."

Let's start here, with a woman I met shortly after beginning this project. We started dating, and I found she had a passion for writing. We have lots of things in common from both business and personal and started talking about this project. Together, we brainstormed on how to make it grow. Part of the authorship program was a trip to Ireland with a group called ENE (Executive Networking Event). As we traveled to Ireland, we sat in airports, restaurants, and cafes talking about Cowboy Warrior Project to everyone we met. Cowboy Warrior Project started out as an idea for a book to tell the story of a process, and as a vehicle to help reach thousands of people. After beginning to write the book, the realization set in that this was much bigger than just a book. We realized this project needed to entail practices of both cowboys and ancient warriors alike. The entire process has led us to many, many new connections.

Upon arrival in Ireland, we shared our idea and concepts about Cowboy Warrior Project with some other business owners from different countries and states. From the collaboration of efforts and strategies of multiple business owners, Cowboy Warrior Project's vision has really grown. While in Ireland, because of the relationships and connections we made, and we gained all tools and people needed, we have fallen and continue to fall into place for the project as though it was meant to be.

As I mentioned above, my daughter struggled in school and was very timid about trying new things. It took me three years to even get her on a horse. I started her on a miniature horse, which she rode for one week, whereto she gained enough confidence to get on a large horse. Three years ago, she started Junior High Rodeo, and in the beginning, she was so nervous she didn't complete the pattern; didn't get a time or score. After the fourth rodeo, she completed the pattern and received her first "score". She continued that year, each rodeo getting faster and faster, and ended up placing in the top 20 out of 138 girls in her event.

At this point, her confidence swelled. Rodeo got easier, school got easier, and life in general got easier. This little girl had been on IEPs (Individual Education Plans) since first grade. Through finding her confidence with her horse in rodeo, as of a few weeks ago, she is now off all of her IEPs. Her reading level has gone up 220% this year. For this reason, I felt this story needed to be told. The practices I have instilled in my children need to be shared. We convey and teach people that through mental toughness, strong work ethic, respect, 'never give up mentality', and a 'plan to win' mindset, they can succeed at anything they set out to do.

Now, through the connections we've made while in Ireland, Cowboy Warrior Project is well on its way to help thousands to millions of people all over the world. We have people in Australia, Ireland, China and the United States all working together to help us help others who need the ancient and forgotten ways.

After twenty-eight years of being a business owner, I've learned that no matter what your business is, it is all about relationships and connections. If you build strong connections and relationships, you will always have clients, and money follows. The magical part of connections is that when you meet that connection, you never know where that connection will take you. I started out with an idea about Cowboy Warrior Project in Idaho Falls, Idaho, and now we have weekly phone calls with people from Ireland to Australia all working to help us get our message out.

At every turn, we meet new people and new opportunities are presented to us. We never know where our next connection may lead us. Meet lots of people, make everyone smile, and leave a powerful impact on everyone you come in touch with. The message you leave with them is the message they'll take away.

JAMES BILLMAN: I'm James Billman with *EXP Realty*, in Idaho Falls, Idaho. I grew up right here in the local community, and have been a business owner for over 28 years. Therefore, I have a larger network than most Realtors you will work with. I focus on getting results and taking care of my customers. The Real Estate business is about creating relationships and trust. With being in business in a local community for 28 years, we've build a positive reputation and earned the trust and respect from customers and peers alike. We also have a multitude of marketing experience and expertise in all areas Real Estate related. Whether you are looking to Buy, Sell, or Invest in residential, farm and ranch, luxury homes, or commercial properties we will help you achieve your goals and would love an opportunity to earn your trust. Every day is a new day in life and in Real Estate. We are looking forward to meeting you, serving you and helping you with any and all of your Real Estate needs. Give us a call today and let us prove to you what sets us apart from the rest.

Connections - My Personal Castle Journey

I'm in a role in work I don't want to be in. Sound familiar? Things changed in my career in 2015. A dramatic event occurred which awakened an opportunity for a business. This opportunity took a few years to germinate, though. I took some time off in February 2019 to process the work event and I discovered my true calling, to become an International Humanitarian. I felt better. I got my confidence back. I believed my day job wouldn't define the rest of my life. The fog cleared in my mind, many tears flowed and the awareness I've so much more to offer the world occurred. I had time to let the seed of realization sprout and discover deep down what I'm supposed to be doing with all my lived experiences as a humanitarian nutritionist from across two continents, Asia and Africa. And hence my transformation began. I reached out and talked to people like me, old connections, and then I made some new connections too. People who saw my vision. People who offered me independent opportunities once they heard my background. One special person was Lisa Strutt, who told me about this amazing one-week event in Crom Castle where I could meet the world-renowned Author Karen McDermott. Part of my business idea is also the creation of my memoir 'My Humanitarian Diaries' from journals I kept to deal with the extreme conditions and scenarios of war-torn and famine-stricken countries. I also heard Shelly Yorgesen, a networking guru, would be there too. The castle sounded exactly what I needed–a confidence and belief missile. My mind ran away with me as I really wanted to fulfill my dream of writing my book and starting my own business. I immediately checked it out and knew it would be amazing, but it was expensive, even for one day. Being the determined and focused lady I am, I moved a few things around. The dramatic change in work had halved my earnings, but the opportunity to be part of this event was priceless. So off I went to Crom Castle after great discussions online with both Karen and Shelly, who seem so authentic and supportive, with no business but with my mind, body, soul, passion and drive to succeed. It was a huge leap of faith, but it has paid off twenty times over in the year after. It took some planning, as I am a mother too, but I was determined to go even after little sleep as my youngest son became violently sick the night and morning of the event. Deep down I was excited and nervous as I knew no one except Lisa, but I realized I would continue to know no one if I didn't step up. My day was priceless. It included 9 15-minute talks and an Authorship Afternoon with

Karen. Both Karen and Shelly greeted me with bear hugs like we are old friends, and I felt safe and welcome in an environment which was so new to me. I was proud of myself as I'd made it. I was in a room full of amazing successful people all networking, enjoying coffee and laughing. I force myself to do the same. Networking isn't something I do naturally, but now in 2020, I have no issues. People from all over the world want to speak to me. I keep eye contact; discuss my business ideas out loud and really connect with some amazing women. I shy away from two men who are sharply dressed, Ron and Mark, as I felt they wouldn't want to speak to me. How utterly wrong was I? The one thing each speaker had in common is authenticity. There are laughs, tears, and so many golden nuggets. They inspired me all morning and when Karen asked if anyone had a book idea; I said mine out loud before my brain caught up with my mouth. My ears were ringing, but I had said it–another leap of faith. The learning from these businessmen and women was outstanding. Over lunch, I made more connections, including the wonderful Sarah Blake. We clicked over our children, two boys each and the same ages. I am inspired that it can be done; be a mother and have a business. It is Authorship time, and I was a little nervous but smiled and breathed. In the session there were people who'd written numerous books, but I stayed focused and calm. I saw interested faces when I discussed my book and felt good. I shared some writing with Karen, and I sat frozen as she read my words. I reminded myself that only I can do this and kept smiling while my head was pounding. Karen smiled and told me to keep going and offered me some priceless advice, and I breathed again. The day was over. I was physically and mentally drained. I am thrilled I pushed myself. I attended as a stranger and left as a friend. I was emotional as I walked away, full of pride, joy and excitement. Pride for going alone, joy as now I have new connections for life, and excitement with a notebook full of wisdom including book advice. A year later and I now have extremely strong global friendships who I learn from and am supported by daily. I also have new connections from the castle connections, and I am a member of the ENE Inner Circle. I have acted out my dream and started my own business in April, Unique New Adventure Ltd, rejoicing in our differences through education. I have delivered expert talks and participated in podcasts, including Shelly's. I am at the beginning of my journey with more adventures to come. I have the utmost confidence in myself that I will succeed in all I create, including being a successful author, making a difference and giving back. I learned that day to connect authentically, and my day at the castle is the gift that keeps on giving both in life and business.

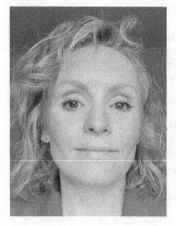

UNA LAPPIN: I am an International Humanitarian. I am married with two boys and I currently live in Belfast, Ireland. I have worked as a Nutritionist and a Consultant across two continents, Asia and Africa, within a variety of countries including Afghanistan, Ethiopia, South Sudan, Iraq and Democratic Republic of Congo where I was responsible for implementing nutrition, health and food security surveys for children under 5 and their mothers, the delivery of targeted feeding programmes and health promotion with *GOAL Global, CONCERN Worldwide, ACTED* and *United Nations World Food Programme*. I am the Founder and Director of my own business, *Unique New Adventure Ltd.* which I established in April 2020 to 'Rejoice in Our Differences Through Education'. I have delivered multiple educational workshops, expert talks, global podcasts, videos, interviews and storytelling from my lived humanitarian experiences. I am looking forward to furthering this continual sharing of my privileged education from across the world with children and adults. I am passionate about sharing my knowledge and experiences of working as a Humanitarian so I'm currently writing my memoirs from daily journals I kept when I worked internationally. I was a community nutritionist researcher within the University of Newcastle upon Tyne in England and locally I have tackled life and health inequalities with Irish Travellers and many communities across Belfast with a focus on mental well-being, food and fuel poverty, homelessness and health literacy. As a result, of my career to date, I have extensive experience in community engagement; locally, nationally and internationally and interacting in a multicultural multidisciplinary environment. I am one of the Directors of *JoinHer Network*, a voluntary member of the *Royal College of General Practitioners NI Patient Group* and a voluntary Ambassador for *CONCERN Worldwide*. I hold a Diploma in Industrial Studies, a BTEC in Community Capacity Building Trainers Programme, a BSc Hons in Food Technology Management from University of Ulster, a Masters Degree of Science in International Nutrition at University of Aberdeen and I am first author in a scientific publication; Tohill, U.R., Curtis, P.J., Adamson, A.J., Mathers, J.C. (2001) *Individual's perception of diet with regard to health compared with recorded intake.* Proceedings of the Nutrition Society. 60, 181A

DALLAS KING

One connection that helped me in business? I have just the one.

How about the one where I met a remarkable mentor and coach who tells it like it is, and isn't afraid of letting me lead?

I met this man on my first networking call. The only woman in a "room". It was on Zoom, full of guys. And not just any guys. Freaking business owners! Guys who had way, way more experience and knowledge of the world I had only barely dipped my toes into. Yeah, that's not intimidating at all.

But I stepped into this network because I wanted to learn from these guys, and I wasn't about to let my own insecurity get in the way. So, I hid behind the 'mute' button and I listened. At least, that was going to be my plan. Apparently, fate had another idea. I was called on to introduce myself to the room before anyone else. I think the exact phrase that went through my head was, "Well, shit." Irony is a major component in my life, it would seem.

"Okay then," I thought. "They want to know why I'm here. I'll just tell it like it is."

I have no idea how it came across to them. I hope it made sense. I hope my sentences were understandable; with a beginning, middle, and end. But the one thing I did that helped the most was to put myself out there with the biggest problem I needed help with. And honestly, it was a problem I didn't think a single one of them could do a damn thing about. I had them stumped, and I knew it.

Except I didn't. The thing I needed at that moment, or at least focused on, was the need to find a buyer for an extensive collection we were trying to sell for a client. The pool of possible buyers was small, at least it seemed that way from our experience up to that point. This was a BIG collection, and not many people in that particular world had the money to make such an investment. And this is where irony caught me again.

Wouldn't you know it, one guy served me my first piece of 'truth pie' in what would eventually become a relationship of pies and conversations I will forever be grateful for. He tilted his head to the left side and said, "Huh. I bet that won't be very hard to get rid of." Just like that. Like turning people's perceptions on their ears was a daily thing for him. Which, now that I think of it, it probably is.

I was flabbergasted. I had nothing to say to that.

So, the call proceeded from there. We're all talking about what we need, what we liked about our businesses, what was going well, etc. All the while I'm sitting there in my head wondering who the hell this guy is and what world he lives in that he thinks something of this magnitude isn't hard to find a buyer for? Seriously?

Fast forward a few hours and I finally had the intestinal

fortitude to message this guy and ask what he meant by that remark? All casual and breezy; not at all self-conscious and unsure of myself, like Monica calling to check Richard's voicemails. I'm sure that's how it went over.

The text I received back was just as forthright as you could expect a reality check to be. "Call me at your convenience." Well, shit. I had to talk to him? As if the zoom call wasn't bad enough, I had to talk to the guy? The one with who knows how much clout and power in his back pocket? Sure, let me just talk to you like you're a normal human being. That's fine.

That phone call was blessedly short and sweet. I asked what he was on about. What did he know, or better yet, *who*, and how do I get a hold of these kinds of people? I got the info I asked for and went along my merry way.

Until the next zoom meeting. He freaking told us point blank that he wanted someone who was serious about showing up for themselves and their business. He wanted them to be as invested in the job of making a go of it as he would be when offering his help.

'Can't get any more direct than that,' I thought. 'Here's goes nothing.' And I called him again. But only after I put on what was clearly not enough deodorant. I tell this Goliath I want to be the one he helps. I want to be successful, I want to be big enough to reach all the people out there I possibly can. And I want to work with the best of the best, and that includes him. And then I passed out. Well, not really, but it was freaking intense! Apparently, I said something intriguing because he tells me what that would entail, and to take the night to think about it.

Slightly worried about what I was getting myself into, I reach out to the leader of this networking group to ask what she suggests I do. Actually, I told her what was said, what I felt, and my crazy idea to offer as a counteroffer, and she told me to go for it. So, I did. But not until the next morning. I'm not up to that much in one day.

Long story short, we made a deal. I had his phone number and his attention for I don't think either of us know for how long. But I had the help I needed. I sent him every crazy idea that popped into my head. I called him with every hang-up and reservation that came across my path. It even got to the point where I was forbidden to buy any more books because I was hiding in them instead of just going out and learning by doing. It was the most exhilarating and exhausting growing experience I'd had with a business ever. Not even new-day-on-the-job jitters compared to this feeling.

Now, I am here, ready to step out on my own without his holding my hand. I feel so confident in all I have learned that I am not even scared of what the road ahead holds for me. At least, not super scared. I know he's going to be there if I need him. Right, Mark?

DALLAS KING is a new and upcoming empowerment coach specializing in helping women and mothers banish their frustration and overwhelm by helping them to rediscover and embrace their power so they can have deep and abiding joy. She enjoys reading, writing obviously, knitting, crocheting, swimming, shopping and being around others to share fun times and deep conversation. Her goals include being able to buy a home somewhere in England, being conversant in French, and being able to shop at Harrod's without worrying about price tags...even if it's for chocolate. She is mother to two teenage boys and finds it both exhilarating and challenging. She and her husband have been married for 17 years and have lived in Wyoming, Idaho and Utah.

Adventures in connecting: A conversation with my daughter

As a leadership coach and adviser, the thing I spend most of my time on with clients is relationships. First, the relationship they have with themselves and second, the relationship they have with others. So, you can imagine when my eldest daughter heads to university to study business management and asks me, "Mum, how can I be sure to make good connections?" that my answer centers upon *relationships*.

I tell her three stories to help her remember what is important.

1. The relationship with your younger self: don't underestimate the power of your own childhood experiences.

Growing up in Belfast, Northern Ireland, in the 1970s, I was gifted a love of books, thanks to Aunt Una who was an avid reader. One of my favorite books was *"The Lion, the Witch and the Wardrobe"* by CS Lewis, who was born not far from where I was raised. At weekends, I would stay overnight at my grandparents' home. Picture it, a huge wooden-framed bed and a fitted wardrobe filled with musty smelling clothes and a selection of fur coats. I truly believed that beyond the fur coats was the magical place called Narnia. In the book, Lewis says, *"Some journeys take us far from home. Some adventures lead us to our destiny."*

What if you learned to think about your life as an adventure?
No daring enterprise would be without its hazards.
No person you encounter would be without value.
No experience, no matter how challenging, would ever be wasted.

New Year's Day, Belfast, 1977
I was five years old. I had been at my grandparents' house for a celebration. As my mum, dad and I returned to our neighborhood, we discovered we were not allowed to enter. They cordoned the street off, and we had to wait for what seemed like an eternity.

Eventually, when we were allowed to return home, we discovered our windows and doors had been shattered. The street was a mess with debris. A bomb had exploded.

It ripped apart our community.

Only with hindsight, I realize what a time of struggle and trauma this was. I see now, my parents' resolve to teach me to look out for others in my community no matter who they were or where they came from. I was taught to serve without expectation, to go the extra mile and to knock on my neighbors' doors to find out if they needed any groceries from the corner shop. It was then I learned that when you give, you often receive. Sometimes, it was as simple as a shiny silver ten pence piece and other times it was a smile, a compliment or a word of encouragement about school.

These values and experiences shaped the person I have become, and they have drawn me to make connections in business with like-minded people; to build community and to give back wherever possible.

2. The relationship with your current self: talk less, listen more, examine your surroundings to uncover a wealth of resources.

You won't find out about others if you are only interested in your own agenda. When you are genuinely curious about other people's values, experiences and motivations, you get to know them, what matters to them and how you can help them. This takes courage. It may feel counter-intuitive: how will you be memorable, if you aren't the one doing all the talking? I can assure you the attention you give to others, enables you to build deeper, more meaningful relationships. This, you will find, brings you happiness and, as a by-product, access to a wonderfully diverse network. There's an old saying that goes something like this, "Most people will forget what you said, but they will remember how you made them feel."

While we were living in Portugal, I was asked to be on the board of an international swim team. For two years, I worked closely with a truly international group of people. We traveled together to competitions in Germany, Italy and Spain. I was simply playing to my strengths: collaborating, connecting, making people feel welcome and part of the swim family.

Yet, from that time in my life I met successful C-suite executives; military spouses who felt like they used to be "a somebody"; ex-pats looking to find more meaning in their lives and soon-to-be veterans exploring new possibilities. I offered mentoring and coaching to help them figure out their next steps. I wasn't aware of it at the time, however, looking back, I see how these experiences took me on the journey of building a prosperous coaching practice. And they planted a seed that six years later grew to become a new business venture, Career Reboot.

Many of the people I got to know then have become lifelong friends, some have become clients and one a business partner.

3. The relationship with your future self: define who you want to become and who will help you get there.

Any good adventure story has those moments when the protagonist has to make some tough choices. Typically, this is to do with legacy. If I were to die right now, what would I be remembered for; what did I stand for; who would mourn my loss? This thought process then sets their moral compass and direction of travel, guiding their decisions for the next leg of the journey. So, who do you want to become and who might help you get there?

Whilst I was looking for resources for coaching ex-pats, I came across Sheryl Sandberg's, "*Lean In*" which is a book dedicated to inspiring women to achieve their ambitions. A question of mammoth proportions is posed: What would you do if you weren't afraid? What a question! It exposed my core fear: failure, and it fired me up to think bigger and set my sights on helping people achieve more than they thought possible. There's no simple hack or fast-track to the destination. Becoming more of who you want to be demands self-discipline, focus and effort.

Within five years:

- I was invited to meet Sheryl Sandberg.
- I became Chair of the Board at *"Lean In Belfast."*
- I went to San Francisco to meet 100 other global Lean In leaders and speak at the event.
- I clocked up over 1000 hours of coaching and became a Fellow at the Institute of Coaching at Harvard McLean Medical School.
- I was recognized by the President of Ireland, Michael D Higgins, for a leadership program for young athletes.
- I met my co-founder for Career Reboot, whom I was introduced to because a mutual connection knew we both cared about equality, learning and development.
- I learned to ask for help. The people in your network can't help you if they don't know what you need or want. This, I've discovered, makes it so much easier to find kindred spirits, the people who join your team, people who want to see you succeed, who become your champions.

So, how can you make good connections? Just as this article is borne out of a conversation, what if you started a conversation with the people you meet? What if that led to an adventure towards your destiny? What would that be worth to you?

LISA STRUTT is a leadership coach, adviser, business growth and development facilitator. Supporting others to add value to their lives and their businesses and create a better future for themselves.

In 2019, she joined forces with the inimitable, Sinead Sharkey-Steenson to found *Career Reboot Ltd,* a company dedicated to supporting career returners with back to work readiness.

She started her career in NI as a Training Manager in the private sector and was thrown in at the deep end of business: selling and delivering training programmes to the enthusiastic and non-motivated alike.

I facilitated cross-community work with young people; developed local and international training programmes for unemployed adults; designed and delivered corporate training plans for private sector clients.

Lisa has worked in 7 countries and enjoys speaking about what she has learned from her experiences. As an international speaker, her style is inclusive, informal and engaging with a focus on action and impact. Key topics: purpose, vision, values, resilience, relationships, networking, coaching.

In coaching, Lisa provides an environment to reflect, focus and soul-search. I coach with a mix of compassion and challenge; helping to address imbalance and unlock potential.

MICHAEL DE HAAN

I have worked with money since I was fifteen in Banking and Financial Planning in Australia. Even though I have 40-plus years' experience with money, it has only been in recent years that I understand the effects our core beliefs and mindset have on the way we experience money, regardless of the amount we earn.

The beliefs and mindset we hold around money can have a significant impact on our own quality of life, especially limiting beliefs which can cause considerable stress. We know that financial stress not only negatively affects our physical well-being, but also our relationships and our communities.

Through my own life experiences, I developed a passion for working with women to empower them to experience both financial independence and confident money behaviors, that enable safety and freedom. Growing up, my father worked two jobs to provide for us, then left my mother and four kids when I was eleven without giving any financial support. My mother was a strong and spirited woman, and I watched her work long hours to provide for us while raising four children on her own. Then at fifteen, we found out my twin sister had been abused, which set her on a path of drugs, mental health issues and not feeling safe or like she had a voice. Sadly, my twin sister took her life at the eighteen which had ongoing effects on both my family and me.

Through my upbringing and my family's struggle for money, I adopted a scarcity mindset that would play out in my own life for years to come, causing severe financial stress. After surviving Stage 5 Prostrate cancer, the breakdown of my 21-year marriage, depression and anxiety, it put me on a path of healing and wanting more joy and less stress in my life. I studied the effects of mindset and core beliefs and turned my life around.

I worked through my challenges and re-built a life with less stress and more joy, including a fulfilling second marriage that is not burdened by financial stress. My journey and overcoming my own challenges led me to want to work with women so they, too, feel financially secure and empowered to live the life they choose.

You only have to look at the statistics to see that women still earn less than men. Australian women make on average 18.8% less than men, with various factors including women taking time off to care for children, parents or family needs, inflexible working conditions, gender discrimination, lower wages for female-dominated industries, etc. The effects can be significant for women, especially if there is an unexpected life event such as divorce or the death of a partner.

These issues add up over time and can affect their financial independence. In fact, women aged over fifty-five are now the fastest-growing cohort at risk of homelessness in Australia, with the census reporting an increase in homelessness of 31% from 2011 to 2016.

My experience working with women supports these statistics. It also highlights a common theme around the emotions they experience concerning money which includes anxiousness, suppression of money related feelings and beliefs, and a dependency on the partner to provide while they look after the children. These behaviors have a significant impact on a woman's ability to be safe and financially independent.

Our programming or subconscious beliefs comes from childhood from ages 0 to 7, where we take in all our surroundings without a filter from our family, friends and society. These can become our subconscious beliefs and behaviors as we grow into adulthood and impact the quality of our lives.

For women, these emotions and beliefs experienced are generally in their subconscious mind. My role as a coach and mentor is to guide the development of awareness by shining a light on the beliefs and behaviors that can create financial stress. I then work with them to build healthier core beliefs that will provide a pathway towards financial independence and freedom.

The coaching and the programs I provide are designed to give an understanding to the way you engage with money, and awareness to your money story. Also, the patterns and behaviors that have shown up that have created financial stress, and the transformation steps to achieve financial freedom.

The result is a conscious and subconscious mind (whole mind) that is aligned with people's hearts and mind and free from money blocks, allowing the fulfillment of their dreams and goals.

My Vision

My mission is to empower 10,000 women to have a healthy relationship with money and to set up structures and support that enable them to make informed decisions to build financial safety and independence.

Empowering women is about them gaining self-confidence in their ability to have financial freedom and the confidence to make the right decisions aligned to their values and goals, regardless of their situation.

Additionally, my goal is to also reduce the alarming increase in homeless women aged over fifty-five in Australia by providing coaching and programs that build a healthier and thriving relationship with themselves and money.

MICK DE HAAN is the Founder of *Care to Grow Pty Ltd*, a firm with a strong history in financial planning and building wealth through property. The business now solely focuses on our client's financial wellbeing and transforming negative financial mindsets and beliefs to help them live their best life. Our vision is to empower people to create more joy, freedom and growth through financial wellbeing because Mick has witnessed and overcome the negative impact of financial stress in his own life.

Powerful Pivotal People

Sometimes it is good to stop and look back over the pathway of your life. Along that way you see the major events in life. There will be the 18th birthday, the 21st and the 50th if you are where I am. There will be the holidays that brought you great joy. And there will also be the sad times when you lost a loved one. World events will stand out in your memory, whether for the good or the bad. I am sure you can remember where you were when the Twin Towers event took place.

Many years ago, I read a book by Charlie "Tremendous" Jones which educated me that there were two things that would change your life for the better, the books you read and the people you meet. I am where I am today because of the books I have read and the people I have met.

As you look over your life, you can see all the people who have impacted on your life. Some for the worst and others to your betterment. One of the greatest impacts on anyone's life is initially their family, and then their friends as they grow and develop over time. At an early stage, you are beginning to be shaped. As a father, I often hear my children saying things that just sound like me.

My first job after leaving school was working in the tyre industry, which lasted for eighteen years. During that time, I met some amazing people who were a great influence on my life and taught me skills for both life and business. One such person was Willian, who became a great mentor and encourager to me over my final years with the firm. He was a person I communicated with regularly and who let you grow and develop in the job. During my time in the company, I also connected with others who were pivotal in my life. One was a client who employed me for eighteen months as he took his company through a lot of change. Another was a customer and supplier who then asked me to come and work in their promotional clothing company. That was a pivot from tyres to clothing.

After a few years of working in the promotional clothing industry, I was introduced to a referral organization called BNI (Business Network International). BNI is an organization where business people come together and generate referrals for one another. This organization gave me the opportunity to connect with local business people and to increase my sales through referral. It is always easier to do business when people understand you and your business where they create meaningful relationships.

BNI is not only a referral organization, but it's an organization that values lifelong learning. There are the books, the podcasts, the BNI University, webinars and the in-person training. Every book, every person and every connection makes a difference. It also gave opportunities to serve others as you grew and developed. I am glad today to say that through BNI I have contacts not only in Northern Ireland but also from across the world. People who are connected through the values they live and do business by.

I am where I am today because of one powerful pivotal person in my life. Julie was a fellow director consultant who recognized me as a person who she felt should become a mentor. She felt I had the ability to see any situation from a helicopter view and help. That was the start of my business of working with other business owners and being a mentor to them. As the business developed over time, I not only helped business owners via mentoring but also helped them through facilitating Business Mastermind Groups with added accountability sessions. Julie not only helped me get involved in a new direction, but she also joined me as a client in one of my Business Mastermind Groups. She has truly been a great friend and encourager over these last number of years. She is a Powerful Pivotal Person in my life and in the lives of others.

As I developed my new business, I rejoined BNI as a member and again reengaged many of the relationships which I had built. After a short time, I was offered the opportunity to look after the franchise area for Northern Ireland. The key person in this was Ewan, who recommended I should look after the region. Because of this, I have had the privilege of supporting members over time through training and having business one to ones which have generated business for them. It is great when you see people benefit and when they have those lightbulb moments.

Life for me is about bringing benefit to others around you. My friend, Gerry, was asked by his father once, "Have you left this house better than you found it?" That is a great question for us all. When people have had an interaction with us, do they leave it feeling they have benefited from the experience? I wonder if I am a Powerful Pivotal Person in the lives of others, my family, my friends, my clients, my suppliers or my community. Are you a Powerful Pivotal Person in the lives of others?

It is good to look back and recognize the people in your life that have made a real difference. Everyone has a William, a Julie or an Ewan in their life who has been a Powerful Pivotal person to them. I am so glad I said thanks to William for what did for me before he died. Gratitude is something we should demonstrate regularly.

We are all connected today, but are we connected? Connected by how we Communicate, by how we Collaborate and by how we Create. We are here today because of the books we have read and the people we have met. People who have been Powerful and Pivotal in our lives.

ANDREW DOBBIN is originally from Bushmills but now lives in Omagh. He moved there to look after *ATS Euromaster*. He is very much a family man - married with 3 children. Omagh is very much his base for work with the community through my church connections. His work takes him throughout Northern Ireland, ROI and GB.

His mission is to provide authentic mentoring individually or in a peer to peer (Mastermind Groups) setting where I enable business owners to develop and grow themselves and in turn their business. His aim is to develop individuals to impact their own life as well as their family and community.

WANI MANLY

"You are potentiality materialized.

Within you dwells the same energetic makeup as everything in this world and beyond.

You are everything.

In being everything, there is nothing you cannot do or have.

You can do and have it all...

The "Beyond your wildest dreams, greater than anything you can comprehend with your human mind," kind of "all," ...

You ARE everything

You ARE an energetic match for everything.

Because you ARE the potentiality of all things.

But then you begin to question it.

With a human mind.

Define it, by human standards,

And doubt it, with human logic.

Unless you can comprehend it... it can't be...

Then you are only a match for what you believe. Because you made it so.

But you were born an energetic match for everything.

And without your observation of it, you still are...

But your observation changes it. Because of your need to comprehend it.

You do not need to create the possibility where you can be, do, and have it all...

You just need to stop the disallowing of it...

It dwells in the field of potentiality like any other outcome...

Without your observation of it... it is perfect, whole, and accessible...

It is our humanity that rearranges our experience of the universe and everything inside it.

We become an energetic match for what we believe is so...

Not because it is difficult to become an energetic match for what we desire...

But because we believe it is so...

That it is difficult, that there is something wrong, that it will take time, that we are not good enough, that there is something we must "do" in order to "be" ...

But it is quite the opposite...

The very potentiality of our becoming was a match for everything...

And the materialization of that potentiality (our birth) was a match for everything...

We were born pure potentiality...

Nothing has changed!

Other than the momentary lapses of time where we question it.

But it is always there.

Right here, right now.

There is nothing to do...

But remember..."

Melanie Ann Layer

I was first introduced to Melanie Ann Layer online through Relationship Coach Shelsey Jarvis. Immediately, I joined Melanie's community on Facebook, the ALPHA Femme Group. When I joined Melanie's ALPHA Femme community of women leaders, entrepreneurs and business owners, the first post I came across was an 87:10-minute video recorded on August 8, 2019, by Melanie. The video which I watched and wept to like a baby on June 3, 2020, was entitled, "What I Actually Did to Turn My Life Around." It told the epic story that made Melanie Ann Layer the woman she is today-multimillionaire iconic leader for some of the most leading coaches and impactful leaders in the online space.

In the video, Melanie, while candidly laying in a bathrobe on her couch shared her story of how on her way to becoming the business leader and influencer she is now. How her journey included her being homeless and sleeping in her car during February, in the middle of winter in Canada. How there were days where she went without food, could not afford minimal gas. And the fateful day when while in this state, living out of her car, became a witness to someone committing suicide jumping out of a building and landing right next to Melanie's car. Melanie also had to declare bankruptcy, yet within the seven years of declaring bankruptcy, became a multimillionaire, recently had her first million dollar month, and is one of the most iconic brands and influencers in the coaching space.

Unbeknownst to me at the time, Melanie is also a high school dropout, which makes her story and this connection even more special. This critical piece of her story would find its way to me three months later, when I would have my first "Melanie Layer Experience," and experience why she was the most adorned leader online.

It occurred during Melanie's 5-Day course E2, which was a course on emotional intelligence and balancing feminine and masculine energies to create the business one desires, become the ultimate leader of leading oneself, and summarily, manifestation. Little did I know when I clicked "I'm In," and submitted my email address to opt into this course, I was stepping into what would become the most defining and transformational moment for the upleveling of my business. That it would quantum leap me into the next version of myself.

Melanie spoke for five consecutive days for a little over an hour each, yet I didn't hear one word Melanie said. Instead, I felt and experienced every single word she said. And, an entire new world opened up to me, a vibrational one that is, and I became the pinnacle realization of her words above. But more specifically, that, "… We ARE an energetic match for everything, because we ARE the potentiality of all things. That we have always been, and nothing has changed, except momentary lapses of time…"

When I felt this, remembered it, instantly, every limitation I once believed in collapsed, including the limitation and fallacy of time. I realized this thing called "Infinite Possibilities," was not some pie in the sky Law of Attraction aspiration, but a palpable truth I had tapped into, and nothing would ever be the same. Life as I knew it was truly over, and this was the rebirth of my business, a new lease on life and everything I wanted to become. Instantly, I became unavailable for anything and everything that wasn't aligned with the truth above, and immediately, the impact was reflected in my business. I landed a corporate endorsement and affiliate for the legal bundles and contract templates produced by my newly formed company, Where Inspiration Meets Law, LLC.

My law firm, W. Manly, P.A., was hired to secure the intellectual property rights of nearly 20,000 rare lost paintings of Holocaust survivor Matthew Troyan. I now wake up to people whom I've never had any interaction with on social media asking how they can send me business, inviting me to speak, collaborations, television appearances, and so much more. The demand for me, my energy, my work and what I have to offer has been such that I've had no time to stop to catch my breath.

In October 2020, I will begin Melanie Ann Layer's year-long flagship program, the ALPHA Femme Experience, which will not only catapult my business, my brand and my impact, but enable me to be the woman and leader I know I am meant to be. So watch this space. And in further words of Melanie Ann Layer, Pineapple season is coming, and it's my favorite season. Harvest time abounds.

WANI IRIS MANLY, (*Esq. W. Manly, P.A. Where Inspiration Meets Law, LLC*) Attorney, Speaker, Bestselling Author & Entrepreneur Wani Iris Manly, Esq. is a corporate, business, securities and trademark law attorney, an inspirational keynote speaker, consultant, and two-time bestselling author. She is the founder of the law firm *W. Manly, P.A.*, a boutique corporate and securities law firm she started in 2008 in Miami, Florida, with offices in Paris, while serving some of the most recognizable companies including, MasterCard Int'l, Inc., Visa, Inc., and Office Depot, Inc., to name a few. Wani is also the founder of *Where Inspiration Meets Law LLC*, which provides legal contracts and document templates for entrepreneurs, coaches, heart-centered and impact driven businesses, and creatives, to legally protect their businesses while fulfilling their purpose-driven mission in the world. Licensed in both the States of Florida and Illinois Wani has over 17 years of international business, corporate law and securities law experience, as well as intellectual property law experience while working exclusively with C-Suite executives of U.S. and foreign public traded companies, small business enterprises, entrepreneurs, individual stockholders and brokerage companies. Wani holds a Juris Doctorate law degree from The John Marshall Law School at Chicago, inclusive of European Comparative Law at the Universita di Parma Facolta di Giurisprudenza in Parma, Italy, and Fundación Universitaria San Pablo - Centro de Estudios Universitarios in Madrid, Spain. Wani also holds a Bachelor of Liberal Arts degree in Government-Political Science from The University of Texas at Austin. She is the bestselling author of *"Get Out Of SURVIVAL MODE And Live the Life You Really Want," "There Is Spirituality And Then There Is Truth,"* (publishing 2020) and is currently writing her third book, *"84 Rue Nollet,"* which depicts the story of her daredevil move to Paris in 2012, a city where Wani knew no one, not one word of French, without a Plan A, B or C, purely on universal signs over the course of a year that lead her to the iconic City of Lights. As a leading global speaker on living life to the fullest, Wani empowers audiences to stop acting as if life is a dress rehearsal, that tomorrow is guaranteed and to instead live the life they really want and to be unapologetic about it. Along with maintaining her law practice and speaking, Wani also consults for French companies and organizations in their humanitarian missions in Africa, and expansion into the U.S. market, and is an Adjunct Professor at the School of Luxury Management at ISEFAC Bachelor, in Paris. More information about Wani and be found at **www.wanimanly. com**. To contact Wani directly, please email her at wmanly@ manlylaw.com.

RON MALHOTRA

It's interesting that so many people talk about the importance of networking and collaborations in business, but it appears many just pay lip service to it. Even the ones who believe in facilitating collaborations or being involved in networking, typically. They don't always go about it the right way now. As somebody who's gone from corporate to being an entrepreneur, I've had the opportunity to build many businesses across the globe, and build multiple brands.

Today, when new and aspiring entrepreneurs ask me how they can grow their business, I always tell them one of the easiest and the fastest ways to grow a business is to nurture relationships and then leverage off them. And this is exactly what I did over the years. I, unconsciously at the time, looked at how my business could serve the needs of other people and then over a period of time, built relationships which resulted in me acquiring clients through referrals and joint venture arrangements, and collaborations, which resulted in me not having to be a significant marketing cost. This is typically associated with acquisition of new clients and something that a lot of businesses simply can't afford, especially when they're starting out.

So, building relationships allowed me to build my business, probably not as rapidly as I would have if I had spent money on advertising. However, it allowed me to build solid foundations in my business and the clients I wanted to work with, resulting in better retention. And therefore, more scalable businesses. Now, unfortunately, many people these days talk about networking as a business growth strategy, but in my experience, it was not a pleasant one for the networking events I attended over the years. It seemed like a self-promotion fest where people would hand you their business cards and maybe engage in some superficial dialogue.

Or they demonstrated a scripted response or interest in your business, when the whole time their intent was promoting their services, and that kind of put me off from networking for a while. I always wondered if networking was something I needed to do, given that collaborations, joint ventures and referrals had been successful for me to build my business. But I certainly found there were many elements of a networking events cringeworthy, for me, anyway. So I got put off by networking.

However, I realized it wasn't networking that was the problem. It was the way the networking was being done. And many times, it was being done without any proper team or structure or facilitation of learning or exchange of experiences. This dawned on me quite recently. In 2019, when I had the privilege of attending an event Shelly organized, and Karen invited me to attend, I observed networking was more than just a group of people coming together and talking about their business.

I experienced a vibrant energy in the networking event Shelly and Karen organized. I observed there was an underlying theme which facilitated learning and an exchange of ideas. And those ideas were discussed with the attendees in mind because those topics were relevant to me as an attendee and of great interest. Now, of course, everyone at the networking event surely would want to promote the business somehow, but what I enjoyed was the fact that there was a genuine interest in learning about other people's businesses and contributing to areas in the business that they were stuck in. I found that to be extremely valuable because it also gave me an opportunity to talk about my business challenges with other business owners from different industries. Different perspectives gave me different ways of thinking, because no matter how experienced you are in business, you have your own blind spots. And I found that extremely valuable.

The amazing thing that came out of it is that I still have relationships with those people, which has never happened to me in a networking event before. I'm still in touch with those people. And clearly that was not a superficial connection, and it wasn't forced. It was something that occurred naturally. But for it to occur naturally, the right environment had to be facilitated. And that's where I realized when networking is done with proper thought and consideration with the attendees' needs in mind, it can result in a wonderfully memorable experience.

So today, of course, I'm a lot more receptive to networking because I have now understood and experienced its power. And I've a new appreciation for what goes into the organization and the conduct of a successful networking event. I'm most grateful for Shelly and Karen for opening my eyes regarding what is possible when networking is done well. And I believe that people who are a part of the community that Shelly has put together are very fortunate indeed.

To be a part of a valuable community of high energy people who are forward looking, coming together regularly to exchange ideas and thoughts with the intent of supporting each other is wonderful. So, thank you to Shelly and Karen for allowing me to be a part of that experience which has left such positive memories and associations around networking. I hope I get opportunities to be a part of their networking initiatives in the future.

RON MALHOTRA is the author of five books, entrepreneur, award-winning wealth planner, success coach, business advisor, and thought-leadership mentor. Ron speaks internationally on topics including success, wealth, influence, and business. His views are highly sought after and have been published across a range of mainstream media. Ron's online content has been viewed more than fifty million times. Ron lives with his wife and daughter in Melbourne, Australia.

ADREA L. PETERS

The Natural Connection

I don't reign from "connected" people. Loners, albeit friendly loners, would be more apt. I don't mingle well. The thought of small talk gives me hives. The words "ice breaker" brings to mind pickaxes and heavy machinery. I spend the bulk, as in most of my time alone with my two dogs.

It is *because of* those traits, not despite them, that I am one of the most connected people I know. My network stretches across borders, religions, cultures, gender, belief systems, and across all limitations. I have an eclectic network that I am endlessly grateful for and humbly honored to nurture and grow each day.

Every client, job, role, gig, deal and invitation I've received has started with a powerful first impression. Not all "Hi's" and "Hello's" are powerful. Most are utterly forgettable or worse, flaccid. I've been offered powerful positions after this kind of "Hello". People suddenly addicted to my energy, my knowledge, my unwavering devotion to what I love, without me doing anything other than feeling it and letting the connection grow without pause or interruption. We don't know each other yet, yet I am intrigued and pleased.

Why get in the way of what comes naturally?

One such connection that comes to mind is of a Chief Information Officer (CIO), who runs large academic information technology departments. He and his department heads hire several people to help him achieve requisite business goals. I am not someone who wants his kind of someone to know my name. See first paragraph. I like to do a kick ass job *anonymously*. I consult. My role is to make my client look good whilst having them feel proud that *they* did all the work. I try not to exist as more than a pleasant apparition.

I have no recollection why I sat before him on this particular day. We hadn't met, though we knew of each other. I was likely invited to advise and offer suggestions on something technical and complicated as I get to do. It does not matter the reason when it comes to connecting, because connection is beyond a vibe thing. Beyond the content of a meeting. Beyond the past. And beyond all limitation.

In connection, we blend. Often unexpectedly.

The words I used suddenly match the words he used. We instantly shared a viewpoint. It was easy. It was believably baffling in its fluidity. And it was poignant. And fun. No drain. No strain. As if we'd met a thousand times before.

Gosh, it's kind of like a great first date.

A powerful connection *is* intimate. Why not expect intimacy in business? Rapport and confidentiality, warmth and understanding, trusted and dear. It's refreshing. It's different. And it's rare to have this in business. May we dare to be rebellious and nurture this kind of true connection in every facet of our lives. Without sex.

We met that first time for *maybe* fifteen minutes. And that was that. A lifetime connection that has served us both. He knows he can hire me, and I will over-deliver. I know I can reach out to him at any time for advice, help, work or a recommendation. When we connect, we talk briefly about what makes us happy: Boston, California, Vermont, food, exercise, family, friends, travel, personal goals, leaving it up to the Universe, and trying to be good people. Our exchanges about specific work are minimal. He says what he needs. I say yes. We both agree with a nod and a laugh and return to our lives.

We have chatted less than twenty hours in our twelve years of connection. We don't hang out and we don't flirt. We rarely text or email and we aren't Facebook friends. We aren't in each other's lives and we don't discuss boundaries because it isn't necessary. Respect is ever-present in this kind of connection. Our powerful synchronicity occurs every time we engage. It is rich and satisfying and has yielded me well over a million dollars.

Connection isn't about who we know, even if that's how it begins.

It relies on how committed we are to honoring our natural instincts.

May we trust what feels natural to us, especially when we head outside our comfort zone and typical types of people. Deep, wondrous, surprisingly satisfying connections emerge, and last in the most extraordinary of circumstance.

May we be brave enough to walk away graciously when the connection simply isn't there.

May we find intimacy in our professional lives because that, my dears, is where magic thrives.

ADREA PETERS is a novelist and screenwriter who dramatically changed her life through her writing.

Adrea also knows how challenging and ambitious it is to walk our talk and love ourselves, yet, it does not stop her from trying every single day.

In addition to her own writing, she has loved mentoring aspiring fiction, memoir and screenwriters. She has presented the concepts of story for about a decade and now as a shareholder in *Making Magic Happen Press*, the beloved publisher of *Truitt Skye*, she continues to work with soon-to-be published and published authors. She also runs a successful business consulting practice focusing on healthcare informatics.

Adrea graduated Outstanding Senior (Valedictorian) from the University of Colorado at Boulder with a Bachelor of Science in News Writing, earned a certificate as a Holistic Nutrition Educator from Bauman College, and was awarded her Master of Arts for Fiction Writing from Seton Hill University. In her sophomore year at undergrad, she completed a Co-op/paid internship:) at Microsoft, where she learned that her mind tends to work like a computer and from there, her ability to learn skyrocketed.

HOLLY HOLLAND

I believe many attendees felt being at a castle was going to be magical. For me, it has revealed so much about my whole life, personally and professionally.

The questions 'What is holding you back?' 'What are you waiting for?' and the answer 'I don't know'. Well, I am excited to tell you that I know the answer now, and it is Honesty. The dance around honesty has been holding me back. I am so grateful to my Castle Family for helping me see it clearly, and for creating a safe space to share.

The reason I joined The Veranda in the first place was for the ability to share and connect on a whole different level with people around the world with honesty. No chain of command, competition, or any of the roadblocks common to many places of employment, was part of the process. Presenting a business need, and having the opportunity to receive immediate feedback on how to solve it, was a different concept from what I had known. Creating the opportunity to write a book in a castle, and then adding it to a powerhouse networking event, was a bonus and the opportunity of a lifetime. Writing has revealed a lot about me and how honesty or lack thereof has shaped my life. There has been an incredible amount of emotion and change, which I am forever grateful for. After all, you can't change something you have tried to ignore.

The Veranda is a different kind of networking. The concept of helping each other has been such a contrast to the usual mindset. It surprised me how many of the same situations arise worldwide. It doesn't matter where we are located or the business we are doing, everyone has them, and we have many solutions to offer each other. Throughout life, there have been many who have intentionally put up blocks. Too much time, thought, energy and emotion have been spent going around them. Roadblocks, in both personal and business, are put up by those that are threatened by other's success. The road blocks have been incredibly heavy. Even my sleep has been threatened by these blocks. I am working on changing the panic attacks' sleeping pattern. I still dream of being held down, so much so that my body can be physically sore from its struggle. With the Veranda and ENE groups, there is no drama, just solutions.

I am working through a lifetime lack of honesty. I am not that buckling under type of person, yet I have been stuck, on hold. What has happened to a society with a blocking mindset, a fear mongering mindset? I have never understood people being unhappy for others. The Veranda went against every concept I had experienced prior.

With one project, the expected outcome was failure from most. With that lack of confidence, I could do nothing else but succeed. I have always had a success mindset. The team worked seamlessly together as the time drew closer to the actual day. Only two were standing in the way at the end, but could not overshadow the amazing work and enthusiasm of the rest of the team. It was successful! There was a cooling period that had to pass by, with ongoing roadblocks that continued to be challenging until the last day. The ending was a complete success. None of the roadblocks ever came to fruition.

Although the success was a good thing, the panic attacks I experienced continued for six months after the project completion. I had not known what they were and had been experiencing them daily for ten months. I am now coming to terms with the issues around honesty years later. All the weight is drifting away. I am facing the changes I need to make with a new set of resources. I will continue to connect and open new doors of opportunity.

I encourage you to evaluate your life like an outsider. Are there things you need to change? I cannot say enough about having an impartial group to bounce ideas off of. I mean people who actually want to see you succeed. It is okay to be happy for others. You are not giving away your power by being happy for them.

What to include or not include in my book has been riding on honesty. Lack of honesty and the dance I have done around it has not 'extinguished me', but it has held me 'hostage' at various stages of my life.

Returning home was hard, knowing how much work needed to be done and deciding how to proceed. I am making choices that I've never made and setting boundaries that are challenging every area of my life. I have much more work to do in these areas. I love including writing, natural solutions and energy into every facet of my life and wellness lifestyle with 'Intention.'

My time at the castle was magical throughout. It wound up with a group of authors. I had an immediate connection with them and realized I was with 'my people'. I had looked for a writing job since completing a blog for my husband's illness. I experienced connection and honesty beyond. Sometimes what we are looking for is right there in front of us. You will know when you have found your people.

HOLLY HOLLAND is a mom to 2 adult sons. She is an author, international speaker and grief coach that helps women create a life after life, lifestyle or job loss. She helps them get moving and is 'Lighting the Path' for them to write and speak their words, encouraging them to *Keep Moving.* Holly will be launching her first book *Keep Moving, Creating a Life After Loss* in 2020. Whether it is grief or something else that is challenging people, it is best to address the issue and give yourself the time you need. It also is equally important to learn how to go on and keep growing. Her grief coaching program, *Keep Moving,* includes monthly support. Individual support is also available.

HEATHER BURGETT

It's All About Who You Know, How You Treat Them & How You Shine Online

It's all about personal relationships.

In Hollywood, you hear these words all the time: "It's all about who you know."

Whether it's helping Madonna at a Premiere Party; waiting to go live at Fox Business News with Jordan Belfort, aka *"The Wolf of Wall Street"*; walking Steven Spielberg down a red carpet; or shaking hands with Sean Connery at a World Premiere, I've rubbed a lot of big elbows in my publicity career path.

Working in entertainment public relations has given me a rare perspective inside a world that many only fantasize about seeing.

I will say that yes, who you know is extremely important. But what's more important is: how you interact, build and nurture your relationships—especially online.

At the age of 25, it was my dream to hop a plane from Boston to Los Angeles and become a film publicist.

I'd read about the illustrious PMK publicist, Pat Kingsley, and how she masterfully represented Tom Cruise in his movie career. The West Coast with its sunny skies and songs like *California Dreamin'* had beckoned to me for years.

When I made it to Hollywood, my first movie junket was for the re-release of Orson Welles' "*A Touch of Evil*" at the Four Seasons Beverly Hills. I was asked to accompany the film's original stars and legendary actors Janet Leigh and Charlton Heston to their individual hotel suites between interview breaks. I practically had to pinch myself when it happened.

They were both pleasant and polite as we made idle chitchat. As the PR rep, you're not supposed to be a fan, but I couldn't help myself. I asked each of them to sign a publicity still from the movie, and to this day, it sits behind my desk as a reminder to the reality I created for myself in becoming an entertainment and film publicist within months of landing in the City of Angels.

This new world was such a deep contrast from the small town where I was raised.

I believe one of the core reasons I stayed so grounded amidst all the glitz and glamor is because of my humble beginnings.

Being raised in a lower middle-class family in a tiny cow town in Western Massachusetts has always been the root of one of my greatest strengths and weaknesses. The people there were kind, honest and good-hearted.

It taught me the deepest of integrity and honesty—and to

always expect the best from people. This can sometimes be a double-edged sword that allows people to try to take advantage of me. But I've often said, "Don't mistake my kindness for weakness."

Within about a year of starting to work in Hollywood, I had the fortune of being a part of the phenomenal journey of "The Blair Witch Project." It was my first big feature film project, and it was an honor to be part of the acclaimed PR campaign.

A year after the roller coaster ride of the film becoming one of the world's most profitable films ever, I left Hollywood to launch my own PR agency at the age of 28.

Those early days of networking and relationship-building were the impetus for me being able to sustain my own business for 20 years—entirely through referrals. I never once needed to enlist advertising or even use my own publicity strategies for my own business.

I nurtured my reputation of high integrity and authenticity through the years, which resulted in a steady flow of new and repeat clients.

I also grew comfortable staying in the shadows while my clients were positioned center stage.

It was only recently, in 2017, when I started teaching publicity via my online PR Stars programs that I started to come out from behind-the-scenes and into high visibility.

That's when I started taking my own medicine to step into the forefront of my business, which was a giant leap of faith. It was terrifying to do it, but it has become easier with every comfort level that I've stretched.

From not wanting to have my photo on my website or thinking I'd never do videos—then flash forward to impromptu Facebook Lives, public speaking, hosting a podcast and running live events, I'm now much more comfortable in the spotlight.

And every time I've put myself out there in a bigger way, I've had new wonderful connections and experiences lead to an up-leveling of my business

With the proliferation of our digital age, it's a necessity to have a dynamic online presence if you want the people who are seeking your help to find you.

People often ask me how I do what I do to get the results I get.

Since I've started coaching heart-centered consultants and creatives to teach them what I know and how to do it for themselves, I've had to find ways to bottle it up and share it.

We all have superpowers, and one of mine is enrolling others in a vision to raise awareness for important initiatives, purposes and messages.

I gravitate to world changers—people who care about social causes and making the world a better place.

So, I often use the example of launching my podcast, "The Shine Strategy," with an all-star guest line-up, including a U.S. Presidential Candidate, an iconic comedian, a reality tv star and an Oscar winner.

I leaned into my resourcefulness and what I call my "shine strategies" to enlist my guests into saying "yes" to a brand new show that hadn't even launched yet—with no track record or episodes in existence yet, and zero metrics for a first-time host (me) who they didn't really know from Adam.

New York Times bestselling author Marianne Williamson was an author idol of mine and she also happened to be running for U.S. President at the time. She was a dream interview that I was determined to book.

Without knowing anyone on her team or how to reach her directly, I put on my private investigator hat and started asking around. I always recommend finding a personal connection, or a "back door," as the best bet for securing a desirable outcome with anyone you want to enroll in your vision.

Through a series of introductions, I finally landed with Marianne's right-hand person—the gatekeeper and woman who manages her entire life and schedule.

I introduced myself and told her I was interested in interviewing Marianne, but that I also understood how busy she must be with her political campaign.

So, I asked if they needed any PR help and offered to see how I could be of service since I am a publicist by trade. I followed my instinct and my genuine passion to support Marianne in getting out her messages about how to heal our struggling and divided nation. To me, that message was more important than my podcast.

Subsequently, I booked Marianne on Spectrum TV News, as well as an appearance on Barbara Boxer's podcast.

And guess what happened next?

I was told that Marianne would be happy to be on my show.

At the time, she was doing major mainstream news appearances like CNN, so I felt completely honored that she agreed to make time for my fledgling homegrown podcast.

The idea of leading with generosity and offering to help others is a much more altruistic approach than going right in for the ask of what you might need or want from someone.

I consider it a kind of karmic cycle. When you do good from a pure-hearted place, others want to do good for you.

I used a similar approach securing Bob Saget to be interviewed. I focused on what I knew was important to him, which happens to be his annual fundraiser for Scleroderma—sadly, the disease that took his sister's life many years ago. His passion for this cause was the focus of our interview.

And as for Nick Vallelonga, who had just come off winning

two Oscars for writing and producing "Green Book," I used my super skill of persistence. I was fortunate enough to meet him at an event and asked him in-person if he'd be interested in being on my show. He had agreed and given me his direct email.

So much of what I do is in the art and science of following-up and riding the line between being persistent and a pest—and not tipping over into pest territory.

My motto is that persistence pays.

I had to reach out to Nick several times. It turned out that he'd been a bit burned by the Oscars press gauntlet and had no desire to do more interviews, so that's why he'd been dragging his feet a bit. I listened to his concerns, and then I assured him that this wouldn't be anything like those other types of interviews. We discussed how his story would inspire my listeners to follow their dreams. Then, he was 100% onboard.

In fact, I also had to stay intently on top of the Marianne interview possibility. It *almost happened* numerous times over two months, and at points, it seemed that it might never happen. But I firmly claimed that it was happening. I stayed true to my belief that it was already done and envisioned seeing her on my show— and sure enough, the vision landed.

It also didn't hurt in all of these cases that I had spent the last couple of years building my online profile so that if anyone were to search my name online, an accurate representation of my brand appears in the top results via a myriad of websites, images, press, podcasts and positive testimonials.

Having an effective online presence is a determining factor for you getting the results you want, especially with high profile talent or VIPs.

The first thing that people do these days is Google you. So, if you're wanting to play in a bigger way in life, you've got to be on the right playing field—and that's online.

Ensuring you have a solid and consistent online presence across all your digital and social platforms is key.

Conveying who you are in a credible way lends instant authority.

So, all the ways in which I've helped my clients over the years are the approaches that I now also use for my own marketing and publicity. I practice what I teach.

The last piece I'll offer is the importance of alignment.

In my 30s, I earned over 500+ hours in training in the healing arts and worked for about five years as a holistic practitioner (while still keeping one foot in my PR work).

I realized when having to create a system to teach what I know that the spiritual aspect of who I am and how I move in the world is completely baked into how I function and achieve impactful results for my clients.

While it's important to be in an aligned place and to nurture personal relationships and connections, it's also important to nurture your own connection to the online Universe.

How are you presenting yourself to the world?

Create an aligned brand and stay true to yourself and your vision.

When you lead with generosity, then use your voice and image to share it far and wide, especially online, it can be miraculous to see what divine opportunities unfold.

They might include things like: awards, invitations to speak at events, TV interviews, being able to raise your prices or command higher fees, partnerships, collaborations with your dream clients, feeling more on purpose, changing lives, and so much more.

This has all happened for me and my clients and students, so I know it can happen for you too.

Keep believing in yourself and what you have to offer people—and confidently put yourself out in front of as many people as possible.

The more you do this, the more you'll stop struggling to find connections. It will allow your audience and destined collaborators to *find you*.

Happy connecting!

HEATHER BURGETT is an award-winning publicist and business strategist. She is the host of *"The Shine Strategy"* podcast, and CEO & founder of *The Burgett Group* and *PR Stars Online Programs.* In the past 20+ years, Heather has represented Grammy® and Oscar® winners, authors, billionaires, celebrities, philanthropists, rockstars and top brands. She now helps soulful consultants and creatives up-level their online presence. Through her programs, they learn to shine their signature gifts into the mainstream spotlight so they get visible, grow a global audience and impact the world with their messages—all without selling their souls. Heather is a recipient of the prestigious PRism Award from the PR Society of America and a Member of the *Forbes Business Council.*

Tracy Meguire

It's All About Who You Know, How You Treat Them & How You Shine Online

I pondered this book's topic for a long time. As it was told to me, "your contribution to the book should be about a connection that evolved your business." So, what does that mean? The most obvious connection is related directly to business...a true business connection. But I think the reason I am struggling with the topic is a personal one. For me, significant connections have evolved my business somewhat indirect by their impact on the personal path of my life as much or more so than an impact on my business.

But, ok, let me start with what the power of connections has meant to me and my business in the direct sense. For many years, personal connections were the lifeblood of my brick and mortar business. They were the primary source of business generation and the most gratifying part of being in business and working with the clients I was privileged to get to know. The reach for these connections was limited geographical location, and since the community in which we did business was somewhat small, so were the connections that could be made.

And then came the ability to connect virtually. My first online networking community shifted the connection paradigm for me and my business. Starting with a live event that was held in another country and brought together people from multiple continents, the power of connection literally changed the trajectory of my life. Suddenly, the ability to meet new friends and business connections was no longer limited to physical proximity. It was also not limited to any particular business or professional. I now had a connection with people that I would have never come into contact with except by virtue of a virtual connection.

My world was bigger, richer, filled with encouragement and support from like-minded people and people from whom I could learn. Having a network like this helped me personally and professionally.

As I mentioned previously, I believe the significant connections I have made, while ultimately benefiting my business, are more complex and intertwined with all aspects of my life. At the end of last year, I made a decision that was a huge life change for me. It would cause upheaval and strained relationships within my family, and it was also a very scary and uncharted course of action for me.

Although I knew it was something I needed to do, I was not sure I had the strength and confidence to go forward with my plan.

During this same year, I became part of a women's virtual networking group. Over the course of my time in the group, I developed some strong, supportive connections with many of the women in the network. The end of 2019 culminated in a live event where many of the women from this group and other men and women from around the globe converged on a castle in Ireland for a week of learning and networking.

The trip was extraordinary, and definitely a once in a lifetime experience! Our week together involved not only sharing on the professional level, but allowed us to spend quality time together; sharing our dreams and passions, laughing and having new experiences, and bonding in a powerful way in a very special place.

So here, on the precipice of an enormous upheaval in my life, I found those who would support and encourage me during this enormous life transition. Friends who gave me strength, who accepted me regardless of the difficult decisions I was making. Women who were there for me and helped me to see I could move forward and thrive personally and in my business. Friends who helped me see that it was ok to want more out of life.

The connections I have made in the networking space, and the support I received from these wonderful people, and continue to receive daily has been positive. Therefore, have had the courage to go forward into my new adventure, positive that it was the right thing and knowing that I can do this! And, because of these connections, I am confidently growing a new business that is allowing me to pursue my passion.

If I hadn't had the connections I made with this wonderful group, I truly believe I would not have made these changes. I wouldn't have found the courage to jump off that cliff and leave everything that was comfortable and familiar behind in pursuit of a life that would light me up. And, in turn, I can offer similar encouragement and support to those I work with in my business.

So, although much of my journey with connection is the story of my personal life, it spills over abundantly to my business life, and ultimately to those I serve in my business. It has made me stronger and more confident, which makes me better at serving my tribe. It has given me the understanding of the power of connections, so I am excited about the opportunities I will have in the future to pay it forward. Without these connections, my business may never have been birthed, and I certainly would not have been equipped to provide the value to my tribe I now believe I possess.

or shaking hands with Sean Connery at a World Premiere, I've rubbed a lot of big elbows in my publicity career path.

Working in entertainment public relations has given me a rare

TRACY MEGUIRE is the owner and CPA of ThriveProfit Pros. With over 35 years experience in public accounting Tracy is experienced in all areas of tax planning and compliance as well as working with entrepreneurs to manage their businesses.

She will help you navigate your personal and business finances. In her life away from taxes, she loves connecting with other women entrepreneurs, is an avid genealogy buff, has recently embarked on learning a foreign language, and adores spending time with her grandson!

CPSIA information can be obtained
at www.ICGtesting.com
Printed in the USA
BVHW031548150222
629077BV00011B/624